Advancing Talent Development

Advancing Talent Development

Steps Toward a T-model Infused Undergraduate Education

Philip Gardner and Heather Maietta

BEP BUSINESS EXPERT PRESS

Advancing Talent Development:
Steps Toward a T-model Infused Undergraduate Education

First published in 2020 by
Business Expert Press, LLC
222 East 46th Street, New York, NY 10017
www.businessexpertpress.com

ISBN-13: 978-1-95152-706-8 (paperback)
ISBN-13: 978-1-95152-707-5 (e-book)

Business Expert Press Service Systems and Innovations in Business and Society Collection

Collection ISSN: 2326-2664 (print)
Collection ISSN: 2326-2699 (electronic)

First edition: 2020

10 9 8 7 6 5 4 3 2 1

Printed in the United States of America.

Abstract

Talent development is key to organizations keeping pace with the rapidly changing social and technological developments of today's workplace. Companies are calling for talent that possesses a mastery of discipline and systems, combined with an ability to handle cross-functional, multicultural teams, projects, and assignments. Colleges and universities face challenges in preparing students across all the competency dimensions employers demand. The T-model configures academic and professional development in a way that allows institutions to provide students with a solid foundation, one built through rich academic and cocurricular experiences that allow them to grow and adapt to the evolving workplace. The T-model comprises five key elements: mastery of academic discipline, system understanding (systems thinking), boundary spanning competencies, interdisciplinary understanding, and a strong sense of self (the ME of the T). In this volume, readers are introduced to the dynamics of the workplace that generate the need for T-professionals, followed by discussion of each of the five key elements of the T-model. Readers are then introduced to and shown how representatives from different segments of higher education infuse the T-model across the curriculum. The book's final section offers insights from industry professionals on the necessity to grow as a T once a new graduate enters the workforce.

Keywords

talent development; T-model or T-professional; undergraduate education; purpose; boundary spanning abilities; systems thinking; future of work; workplace competencies

Contents

Foreword

Preparing the Next Generation of Learners

Thanks to my IBM colleagues and the editors for an opportunity to share on the topic of this book from an industry perspective. Advancing talent development is central to my role as Vice President, Chief Leadership, Learning and Inclusion Officer at IBM, and it's an exciting time to reimagine learning for the world that's emerging around us.

The rate and pace of innovation is accelerating, putting significant pressure on organizations to reinvent themselves and embrace new technologies, skills, and ways of working. For customers, their last best experience becomes the baseline for all future decisions and experiences, raising the bar for all companies to deliver a superior user experience every time. With increased competition from new and different sources, organizations are challenged to react in real time, scaling new concepts not featured in their strategic plans without waiting for the annual budgeting cycle. Speed and innovation are the new currencies, which have significant implications for the skills companies and workers need to compete.

We've heard from CEOs globally that *talent is the new enterprise risk*, and as many as 81 percent of executives say *talent is the number one priority* at their company (LinkedIn Learning 2018). A 2018 Conference Board study found that "failure to attract and retain top talent" is now the No. 1 issue on the minds of CEOs, even more important than competition or the disruptive nature of technology. However, according to a 2018 IBM study, just 11 percent of Chief Human Resource Officers report their organizations have the necessary technical, domain, and soft skills needed today. To add to the complexity, slightly less than 35 percent of corporations feel new recruits are well prepared with both hard and soft skills to perform at a high level in a professional environment (Workday and Bloomberg 2018).

This collection offers us a blueprint for investment in building a skills profile for today and tomorrow, creating T-professionals with depth, breadth, and passionate commitment to continuous learning. Why does the rate and pace of innovation demand a T-professional? Dynamic technologies and best practices require people deeply skilled in what is new and cutting edge, from cloud computing to artificial intelligence to quantum computing. But technical or discipline-specific skills are not enough. The broad axis of the T ensures an ability to communicate and work effectively in diverse, cross-functional teams in an agile and innovative context. Further, competing on the edge of innovation requires leaders who can create a shared vision, bringing people together to deliver their individual and collective best toward that result. The most skilled leaders know how to tap into the passion of others and ensure employees are fully included and engaged. As a leader, it's my job to set the tone for this level of trust, collaboration, risk-taking, and learning. One example is our *Positive Leadership Edge* program, which helps leaders understand, support, and challenge themselves and their teams, fostering growth mindset and resilience. In this book, that is called the ME in the T, which translates to better knowledge of oneself.

Finally, continuous learning is a long-standing company priority at IBM, and now this is true everywhere. Stand still and you will be disrupted. This is true of companies and individuals as well. IBM has been number one in patents produced by a single company for over a quarter of a century, and now with the acquisition of Red Hat, IBM is also number one in open source contributions. We hire for learning agility, and we're moving from episodic learning to a culture of continuous learning. We offer rich, personalized learning through our *Your Learning* platform, an AI-driven digital learning experience where IBMers can identify and develop "hot skills"—such as artificial intelligence, security, blockchain, project management, agility, and design thinking—to build their future careers.

This book offers powerful insights for the advancement of talent development. As educators and professionals working to prepare and continuously engage diverse populations of students and young talent for the future, I urge you to consider carefully these approaches to infuse the T-model into undergraduate education. Our future depends on it. Advancing talent development is the shared responsibility of great companies and great universities. We are in this together. And together, we can prepare the next generation of learners with the depth, breadth, and commitment to continuous learning needed to stay on the innovation edge.

Deb Bubb

Vice President, Human Resources

IBM Chief Leadership, Learning and Inclusion Officer

Becoming an Adaptive Innovator

My IBM colleagues who contributed chapters to this book, Jim Spohrer, Jana Jenkins, and Richard Hopkins, invited me on behalf of the editors Philip Gardner and Heather Maietta to provide a short foreword. They asked me to offer my perspective on the topic of this book from an IBM and industry perspective, and I am delighted to share a few thoughts.

The digital economy is driving a profound disruption in the world, powered by AI, big data, and cloud computing. As technology evolves, so does the need for new skills. In fact, over the next three years, as many as 120 million workers in the world's 10 largest economies may need to be retrained or reskilled because of AI and intelligent automation. Many of these jobs, in areas like AI and cloud computing, don't necessarily require a four-year degree. IBM's CEO Ginni Rometty talks about new roles emerging in our industry. These aren't traditional blue-collar or white-collar roles but "new collar" roles. New collar is about skills and not degrees, seeking people who are lifelong learners and can quickly adapt to ever-changing technology-driven opportunities.

As we've seen with new collar roles, learning agility can be enhanced with an appropriate college education, but it's not necessary. What is essential is captured in the concept of T-professionals who are adaptive innovators. The ability to learn and adapt to technology-driven change requires quickly developing deeper experiences. It requires a self-discipline of continuous learning and personal reinvention recognizing the environment is ever changing.

Creating new roles and being entrepreneurial are increasingly important skills. T-adaptive innovators make good entrepreneurs because they are ever-inquisitive in understanding and solving customer challenges through agile methods and teaming. In organizations of every size, the continuous transformation of work processes enabled by technological advances create new challenges and opportunities.

Identifying and seizing opportunities also make up the profile of a T-adaptive innovator. Understanding a wide range of disciplines, including management, communications, engineering, and verticals like transportation, health care, and finance are essential to rapid learning and adaptability. As systems become increasingly complex, the ability to look at them from multiple disciplinary perspective as well as see connections between different industries is what sets T-adaptive innovators apart from narrowly focused specialists.

Long-term success requires a deeper understanding of one's strengths and weaknesses. We must be clear on what we are great at, and our developmental opportunities. This is called the ME in the T. There are many ways to assess personality, mindset, skills, and knowledge. However, to truly develop the ME in the T requires real-life project experience—something no classroom can offer. The best way to develop the ME in the T is to explore and expand one's horizons. IBM has a pro bono program called Corporate Service Corps, which is our version of the Peace Corps. Each year, hundreds of our IBMers are deployed around the world, from Ghana to Peru to the Philippines, to volunteer in communities facing difficult challenges. These employees have the opportunity to work with local organizations on high-priority issues such as education, health, and economic development. Some of our IBMers who've had the most rewarding journeys see the world through a different lens resulting from these global assignments. They have returned to their teams and clients with new perspectives.

Finally, I want to reflect on my own experiences of growing as a T-professional. I see it not as a simple straight line. There is no one set path. The diversity of experiences throughout my entire career has helped me become more T-focused. How is it possible for us to develop our T and help our organizations infuse this into the culture? This book will shed light on how you can be a more T-adaptive innovator now and in the future.

Obed Louissaint
IBM VP of Talent

Introduction

Grasping the Foundations for Understanding the T-professional Model

Philip Gardner and James Spohrer

Introduction

The rapid expansion of computer technology into all facets of our lives prompted David Guest (1991), a prominent technology consultant and observer, to advocate for a different type of computer professional that he described as a T-professional: a rounded personality sought in other branches of the same theory, which prizes individuals known as T-people. Tim Brown of IDEO, an early disciple of the T, strongly argued for the T-professional who has principal skill areas or expertise augmented by an ability to branch to other skills (Brown 2005, 2009, 2010). The advantage of the T is having an individual who could explore, gain insight form different perspectives, innovate solutions, and perform in different contexts or environments (Donofrio, 2016).

Also at IBM, one of the authors of this introductory chapter and his colleagues—in developing their theoretical foundation for service science—recognized the importance of identifying the characteristics of professionals who can perform at a high level in service systems (Chesbrough and Spohrer 2006; Maglio and Spohrer 2008; Donofrio, Sanchez, and Spohrer 2010; Maglio, Kieliszewski, and Spohrer 2010). They integrated the concept of T-adaptive innovators into their comprehensive service science initiative (IfM, IBM 2008; Moghaddam et al.

2018). Their efforts brought the T to the attention of engineering, computer science, and management faculty and students around the world (Moghaddam et al. 2016). From these early stirrings, the T began to creep into broader discussions throughout the higher education community.

A fortuitous partnership between Michigan State University and IBM generated wider enthusiasm among higher education institutions for the potential of the T to serve as a constructive model around the design of visionary new forms of curriculum and instruction, coupled with the application of evidenced-based practices for teaching and learning. The T-model triggered conversations on the degree to which innovative approaches to learning design encompass alternatives for shaping and aligning the talent between the higher education experience and post-graduation opportunities.

Three T-summits (tsummit.org) hosted by Michigan State University and IBM gathered industry and education professionals to discuss innovative ideas for integrating the T-model into undergraduate education. The discussions proved engaging and motivating, prompting action within the classroom and across the entire campus. These discussions failed, however, to establish a common language around the components of the T-model. This failure was partially addressed through the monograph, *Primer on the T-professional* (Estry and Gardner 2017).

The contributions to this book build upon the basics laid out in the Estry and Gardner monograph with more attention given to describing the elements of the T with special emphasis on systems/systems thinking and the ME (purpose, confidence, and awareness). The forthcoming chapters will introduce readers to different approaches for integrating the T-concept into the classroom and across the entire campus. Employers share their perspective on the importance of the T-professional in shaping talent development in their organizations.

Overview of Chapters

This book has been designed as a primer for individuals and organizations preparing young talent for the future workforce, especially for faculty, administrators, and professional staff throughout higher education. The opening chapter lays out the origins and impetus behind the T-model and its importance to higher education as a guide to strengthening liberal education, followed by the work of various advocates of the T-model, who have provided insights on working within the T-model framework.

The first part of this volume establishes the framework for the T by delving into each of its major components. To begin with, Estry presents an overview of disciplinary mastery and engagement with other disciplines followed by Gardner and Maietta who introduce systems and systems thinking, and the challenges this component may present education institutions. Drysdale and Rowe then offer a thoughtful discussion on the role and importance of boundary spanning abilities. Part I concludes with Hunsaker and Rivera's insights on the ME component of the T, which comprises three key elements: purpose, confidence, and awareness.

Part II, the main section of the book, provides snapshots of initiatives at different campuses attempting to cultivate the T-model in various corners of the university. The part begins with Grabill expressing the wide door the T opens by designing and participating in learning experiences that bring together multiple agents both on and off campus. The important observation from Grabill and colleagues' work is that students take ownership of their experiences, designing their own learning using the ME element of the T. The part then highlights the work of Savoca and Bishop, who present examples of high-impact practices where the silos between academic services and student affairs are eased. The work of Harding and Krebs at the University of Tampa shows that embracing the T can result in campuswide initiative that engages faculty, professional staff, and the community in a concerted effort to prepare each student to be ready to engage in professional practice. The second part continues with several authors sharing their personal efforts to integrate the T from Sanderlin's initiative to engage first generation, underrepresented freshman in conversations about their purpose; to Martin and Rees's use of the T to stimulate self-reflection in experiential education (cooperative education); and finally, Simmons's inclusion of a T-mindset within engineering courses. Feller and Franklin conclude Part II by tackling the important question of assessing T-development. The authors highlight their work with narrative assessment (storytelling), which offers an exciting approach to integrate personal experiences into one's T-story.

Moving on to Part III, employers share their insights on the importance of developing strong T-attributes for young adults. Archer kicks off the part by presenting why recruiting has changed for Excella's team as they seek emerging T-talent for their internship program and full-time positions, and advocates for strong mentorship opportunities once young adults join the organization. Jenkins examines the several approaches that IBM uses to develop T-characteristics in their staff and Ferguson sheds light on the importance of the T to the development of young leaders in rapidly changing organizational environments. Hopkins concludes with an urgent call to universities to keep pace as the workplace is changing so fast that a T-professional today is going to be morphed into someone more complex within a few short years. He provides examples of the emergence of new professional configurations, all stemming from the basic T-model.

The T-professional

The T-professional, often illustrated as a large block T (Figure 0.1), integrates both depth and breadth. Depth is defined in terms of disciplinary knowledge—ability to understand how individuals with that knowledge function and interact to accomplish a desired outcome within or across a system(s). Breadth, on the other hand, is defined as possessing the professional abilities that allow someone with profound disciplinary knowledge to interact meaningfully with others with different disciplinary knowledge in order to affect an outcome that might not otherwise be possible.

Between Order and Disruption

As disruption and order collide, questions arise as to the existence of a space or zone between the two where individuals can maneuver toward, occupy, and thus, adapt to meet the challenging demands of their work assignment and more importantly, long term, navigate the changes swirling through the workplace. Several conceptual models, using different disciplinary and theoretical lens, have called for such a space. Employing these models in our discussion can assist in framing our responses to technological disruption that demand individuals to be adaptive and innovative.

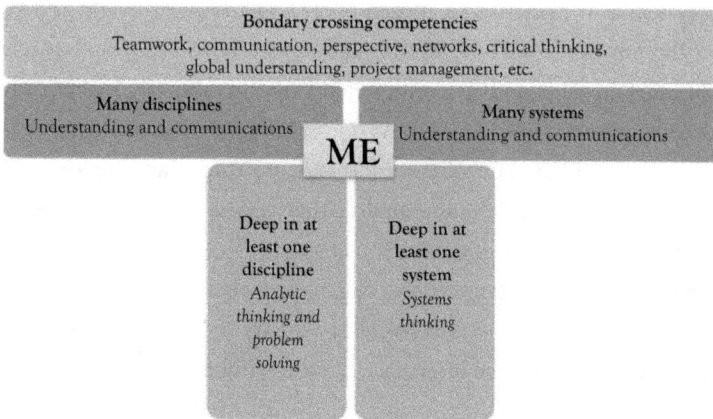

Figure 0.1 *T-model and its components*

Zone of proximal development (ZPD): Educators suggest that a *sweet spot* exists between what a student can and cannot do independently (Krestrick 2012). Vygotsky advanced the concept referred to as the zone of proximal development (ZPD) where students can learn with the assistance of others: "the distance between the actual developmental level as determined by independent problem solving and the level of potential development as determined through problem solving under adult guidance, or in collaboration with more capable peers" (Vygotsky 1978, p. 39). More recently, ZPD became associated with scaffolding or guided learning where assistance and support from mentors, coaches, teachers, and peers aids a learner in mastering tasks beyond their current abilities. This support tapers off as the learner gains confidence and completes the task on one's own.

ZPD suggests a space where learners unfamiliar with an environment (such as the workplace), or how to apply their learning to unfamiliar tasks, can enter the "zone" to find the resources, learning opportunities, and guidance necessary to gain mastery. In the work environment, a mentor or supervisor guiding an intern, for example, can boost professional mastery, establishing equilibrium in disruptive situations.

On the edge of chaos: Waldrop (1992) chronicles the emerging thoughts and experiments around complexity (chaos) theory by scientists at the Santa Fe Institute, particularly Stuart Kauffman (1996) and W. Brian Arthur (2014). Complexity theory provides a window to the behavior of a system as it maneuvers between order and chaos. As Briggs and Peat (1989) point out, "We have traditionally appreciated the simple regularity of order in our familiar world, neglecting the infinitely higher orders (chaos) woven within it" (p. 76). As our orderly practices are disrupted—thrown into a high state of disorder—we are unprepared to deal with the uncertainty, confusion, and anxiety that disorder produces before the system returns to order in a different space.

It is not our intention to delve deeply into chaos theory in this short chapter, but several constructs of chaos theory are necessary to understand how to navigate the interspace between order and chaos:

- *Attractors*: Attractors are events or objects that penetrate an orderly system, creating pressure that eventually sends the system into a state of disorder, triggering self-organization into new order. In our context, we can view attractors as technologies that have been designed to replace workers or significantly augment their ability to perform tasks.
- *Intermittency*: Intermittency interspersed among chaos are islands of order that can aid in reducing uncertainty as order is reestablished. In the context of job disruption, these islands can be the individual's adaptive abilities, which recognize the possibilities emerging out of chaos.
- *Equilibrium and disequilibrium*: An orderly system, considered in equilibrium, is broken apart into a multitude of pieces where disequilibrium reigns. Along the edge of chaos, order is being formed into new systems. Since chaos theory is driven by nonlinearity (Kauffman 1996; Briggs and Peat 1989), small events can have large consequences, creating multiple pockets of order. For an occupation that attracts cognitive systems (software to robotics, for example) the individuals disrupted will have difficulty reconnecting to work unless they can take advantage of new occupational order in another location or space.
- *Feedback*: In nonlinear systems, feedback is critical to sustaining the system and most systems have multiple positive and negative feedback loops. Feedback can amplify fluctuations

in a system as well as mute potential disruptions. Feedback loops can provide inputs to prepare individuals for change by making them aware of potential new opportunities. However, negative feedback can cause roadblocks or resistance to change, which leads to attempts to thwart the adoption of technology or the relocation of facilities to low-cost labor centers.

- *Self-organization*: For order to reassert itself, it is critical that the smaller pieces that move in a disorderly fashion be able to interact to self-organize into some form of order or coordinated effort. Self-organization depends on nonlinearity, a balance of exploitation and exploration (March 1991), and multiple interactions. For individuals who have lost their position due to disruption or in preparing students for lives of disruption, learning takes on a strong ZPD aspect, causing a need to learn from others who have more or different experiences, subsequently creating learning situations that are relevant, meaningful, and effective for the learner.

Visualizing this space between order and disorder emerged through interactions with a grandson of one of the authors who builds elaborate Lego block models (Kauffman also talks about formal and random building blocks). He has built up his confidence by constructing small kits that come with simple instructions, allowing him to quickly move to elaborate models with thousands of pieces. He was comfortable doing this process over and over again. Eventually, all the models were disassembled and the individual blocks place in large bins, the challenge now being to create new models from the 10,000s of blocks available to him without instructions. Here, the grandson struggles until he begins to recognize small patterns and reassemble them into bigger figures, eventually creating something unique. To reach this level of mastery, he trolled YouTube videos, seeing how others created structures from scratch, and attended several Lego groups, talking and exploring ideas with others who have more experience. Moving from orderly, prescribed learning (instructions provided) into chaos where he pursued learning that was meaningful to him allowed him to reassert order.

Pushing this slightly beyond the world of an eight-year-old grandson by considering a disordered state where Legos are flying around amidst Lincoln Logs, Tinker Toys, and other construction materials to gain equilibrium in this system, one must find innovative approaches to use disparate pieces in new ways to establish order. Bringing order out of chaos is challenging, but order will eventually happen if one draws upon their abilities and takes advantage of new learning environments that may be more responsive to one's needs than their current attending environments.

The role of chaos theory is not unknown to those operating in the career development space. Pryor and Bright (2011) delved deeply into how career development can respond to high levels of uncertainty. They lend strong support for the career guidance individuals need that is focused on purpose, confidence, and awareness. The authors neglect, however, the organizational arrangements essential to provide the educational and learning environments that prepare students for disruption. Just as individual counselors need to adopt new insights and methods for guiding clients, universities have a responsibility for creating learning environments and engagement activities that support exploration in an uncertain and unpredictable world.

These different perspectives open a window into assisting students' preparation for and adjustment to changes throughout their working life. Briggs and Peat (1989) confirm this when they state: "Our very life and health depends upon living within layers of order and disorder" (p. 76). To move into this space, we must understand not only the type of working professional that can adapt to changing situations, but also the type of educational support necessary to leverage their learning in adaptive situations.

The Advance of Technological Disruptions

Examine anyone's work history and it is replete with planned and unplanned job changes. Each of us has experienced a job change that was anticipated, allowing time to plan, and thus reducing the transition's impact. The transition from college into the workforce is an anticipated event (Schlossberg 1984) and with proper planning, it can be executed successfully. Other anticipated job moves can be scheduled promotions, planned job changes, or even retirement. Other, more serendipitous moves may come with no prior warning, allowing for little planning. A connection through LinkedIn or a headhunter reaching out with an offer may find you passive in anticipating a job change, but your interest is peaked and may lead to something new. Unanticipated events (Schlossberg 1984) are not scheduled or planned and may result in termination of employment or reduced hours/compensation, thrusting employees into chaos. Downturns in the business cycle (recessions) also come unexpectedly and, since 1990, have caused serious disruption across the workforce. Technology, another source of workforce disruption, is not episodic but rather triggering realignment of work and workers at an exponentially accelerated pace.

Technological changes contribute to perceptions of a widening skills and competencies gap, causing shifts in recruiting mindset toward nurturing talent and the pursuit of more innovative strategies to engage in meaningful enterprises. Technological advances of all types are possible, but this chapter is especially focused on cognitive systems (robotics, advanced software, learning machines, and other forms of AI) because of the constant disruption they portend for workers at all levels throughout the workplace (Brynjolsson and McAfee 2014; Ford 2015; Mindell 2015; Hill 2015). Whether technology simply augments a human's ability to perform tasks more efficiently or replaces humans entirely, technological augmentation of the workplace will be pervasive and chaos-driven (Rouse and Spohrer 2018). To remain engaged in the workplace demands diligence from individuals who are aware of these potential shifts and who can respond adaptively and innovatively to new, advanced technologies.

Perspectives on the implications of smart technologies and work run the gamut from bright optimism about the future of mankind and machines as they become more singular (Kurzweil 1990, 2005), allowing humans the ability to advance economically (Kelly and Hamm 2013; Dormehl 2016) to strong pessimism as smart machines replace many workers and a very few individuals capture machine-driven profits (Brent, Gupta, and Sommer 2013; Webb 2019). It is hard to find a balanced examination of the benefits and costs of rapid technological adaptations in the workplace. Yet, we must acknowledge the ramifications of technology's impact on work.

Consequences of technological change vary depending on which tasks are affected, the timing, and the location of alternative employment. Katz and Margo (2014) provide a historical view of the pervasiveness of technological change in the United States. Technology hollows out jobs, which results in positions being created that require more skills and others that require lower skills. This hollowing out process is described by Friedman (2016) when he depicts technology as pulling jobs apart where high-value elements are skilled up and low-value elements that are:

1. pulled out: where cognitive software and robotics do the entire job and
2. pulled down: requiring less skills and eventually the job becomes obsolete.

Friedman is less sanguine than others who espouse the equilibrium perspective (jobs destroyed equal jobs created). Kurzweil (1990) and Brynjolfsson and McAfee (2012) expressed initial confidence that technology will not destroy jobs to such an extent that many workers will be unemployed may now have second thoughts (Brynjolfsson and McAfee 2014). In fact, Kelly and Hamm (2013), who argue the merits of cognitive computing, believe that cognitive computing will bring a jobs renaissance. The renaissance comes with a caveat in that workers will probably need not only additional, but higher-level skills and must relocate to where new jobs are emerging.

Other observers are more pessimistic (Gada 2016; Johnson 2015). Because the adoption of cognitive systems is moving so quickly more sectors, occupations, and businesses are being transformed than expected. Not only will low skilled, repetitive jobs be lost to technology, but many high-skilled occupations will be realigned, transformed, or eliminated (Webb 2019). Equilibrium will not be easily attained; there will be winners and losers. As both Webb (2019) and Brent, Gupta, and Sommer (2013) imply, the real winners are those who control the technology. We all need to realize that technological disruptions are no longer rare events separated in space and time.

Mindell (2015) makes a poignant comment that astutely captures the effect of technology on work, which we have adapted here:

- Change the technology and you change the tasks.
- Change the tasks and you change the nature of the work.
- Change the work and you change the type of worker required.
- Change enough of the workers and the organization changes.
- Change the organization and you change how the system they are in operates.

The message is clear. Workers at all levels must be able to adapt quickly to technological disruption and innovatively engage in strategies to handle the chaos they find themselves in. The label given to the T-professional, *adaptive innovator*, fittingly expresses the value of leveraging the T-model principles throughout undergraduate education (IfM, IBM 2008). The value being conveyed rests to some degree (but not entirely) on the skills, abilities, behaviors, and attitudes learned and modeled in the undergraduate experience.

Underlying Skills and Competencies in Today's Volatile World

In today's volatile world, corporations are producing advanced technologies that are simultaneously transforming the work processes inside them and between them, including job roles and skills required for success. The crux (core or heart) for T-inclusion in undergraduate education is to provide a meaningful framework for organizing the expanding skill and competency requirements being asked of graduating students by employers. The skill sets cluster around those drawn from disciplinary mastery as well as skills necessary to engage broadly with different functional areas and constituents in the workplace.

Our exploration of the push for additional skills can begin almost at any time post–World War II, but the acceleration began near the end of the 1980s with the recognition that the economy was reorienting globally. At the same time Guest (1991) announced the need for T-people, the Department of Labor Secretary's Commission on Achieving Necessary Skills (Secretary's Commission on Achieving Necessary Skills 1991) focused more explicitly on identifying foundational skills and workplace competencies deemed necessary for graduates to succeed and contribute in the workplace. Foundational skills included:

- *Basic*: Listening, speaking, quantitative literacy, writing, and reading
- *Thinking*: Creative reasoning, making decisions, solving problems, seeing things in the mind's eye, knowing how to learn
- *Personal Qualities*: Individual responsibility, self-esteem, sociability, self-management, and integrity

Workplace competencies included:

- *Resources*: Identifies, organizes, plans, and allocates (time, fiscal, material, human) resources appropriately and logically
- *Interpersonal*: Effective team player, able to teach others, serves clients/ customers, exercises leadership skills, negotiates, works well with people from culturally diverse backgrounds
- *Information*: Acquires and evaluates information, organizes and maintains files, interprets and communicates data, uses technology to process information
- *Systems*: Knows how social, organizational, and technological systems work and operates effectively with them; monitoring and correcting performance; designing/improving systems
- *Technology*: Selecting equipment and tools, applying technology to tasks, maintaining and troubleshooting technologies

Over the ensuing three decades, numerous organizations, researchers, and business associations have pushed an ever lengthening list of necessary skills and competencies to fill the new college gap. These presentations are almost always cast as deficit-based. Even with the addition of more skills or the renaming of these skills, the basic core essentially remained the same.

We could draw into this discussion a lengthy list of studies on the skills gap or changing requirements for employment, but instead will focus on three studies because of their contribution to understanding the T. During the release and subsequent discussion of the

SCANS report, Kelley and Caplan (1993) were simultaneously investigating the performance of engineers and computer scientists at Bell Laboratories. Their research identified the qualities correlated with highly productive, innovative employees—a class of professional they dubbed star performers. Star performers possessed three critical core competencies:

1. The mastery of their discipline (deep learning)
2. Higher-level cognitive abilities (critical thinking)
3. The ability to demonstrate initiative

These core strategies were supported and enhanced by communication skills for persuading others, self-management, leadership, followership, teamwork, perspective, and—even before the social media revolution that delivered Facebook and LinkedIn—networks (or social capital). Kelly and Caplan (1993) defined these supporting strategies as follows:

- *Taking initiative*: Accepting responsibility above and beyond your stated job, volunteering for additional activities, and promoting new ideas
- *Networking*: Getting direct and immediate access to coworkers with technical expertise and sharing your own knowledge with those who need it
- *Self-management*: Regulating your own work commitments, time, performance level, and career
- *Teamwork*: Assuming joint responsibility for work activities, coordinating efforts, and effectiveness accomplishing shared goals with coworkers
- *Leadership*: Formulating, starting, and building consensus on common goals and working to accomplish them
- *Followership*: Helping the leader accomplish the organization's goals and thinking for yourself rather than relying solely on managerial direction
- *Perspective*: Seeing your job in its larger context and taking on other viewpoints like those of the customer, manager, and work team

- *Show-and-tell*: Presenting your ideas persuasively in written or oral form
- *Organizational savvy*: Navigating the competing interests in an organization, be they individual or group, to promote cooperation, address conflicts, and get things done

In a report released in 2010, the Collegiate Employment Research Institute (CERI) focused attention on the changing demands for skills and competencies throughout the workplace (Hanneman and Gardner 2010). Researchers first compared job postings over a 10-year period, the results showing that the starting positions for new graduates in 2007 more closely resembled Kelly and Caplan's star performers than starting position requirements in 2000. In the second part of the study, employers were surveyed as to speed or pace with which certain skills, abilities, work attitudes, and behaviors were changing, and the importance placed on each during the recruiting process. Between 2000 and 2010, seven competencies showed the largest growth in importance among a set of some 20 competencies. They were as follows:

- Build and sustain professional working relationships
- Analyze, evaluate, and interpret data
- Engage in continuous learning
- Communicate through justification and persuasion
- Plan and manage a project
- Create new knowledge/ideas
- Gain a global/cultural awareness

One observation from this study suggests that the total bundle of skills and competencies that employers desire may not really change over time. All skills remain important, but at any one period of time employers may focus on a subset of skills to accommodate changes in technology, labor markets, and organizational strategy. What happens during these changes is a realignment on skill demands that emphasizes different combinations of skills and competencies—stretching or pulling some skills out of the bundle, giving them relatively more importance while others that have been important recede back into the bundle. This shift grabs our attention with reactions likely calling for better prepared graduates.

When industries begin to undergo shifts, employees are responsible to navigating to new positions or opportunities. This requires a shift in job-seeking mindset that is unfamiliar to the majority of professionals. Anchoring their work in the film industry (populated largely by free agents), Jones and DeFillippi (1996) describe a *boundaryless network organization* in which fewer workers expect to spend an entire career within a handful of organizations. Using Kipling's (1902) couplet about the *six honest serving-men* who taught their master all he knew, Jones and DeFillippi identify six factors needed to survive in a boundaryless system in which "people move among firms for projects, develop market niches rooted in competencies, and create opportunities based on prior performance and networks of professional contacts" (pp. 89–90). Three factors concern the individual (*why, whom, and how*) and three factors relate to the industry (*what, where, and when*):

- *Knowing why*: Meaning, motives, purpose for pursuing a career, know values and goals, which allow for the pursuit of passion
- *Knowing whom*: Creating and sustaining relationships (social capital) to create opportunities and provide resources, gaining mastery of knowledge of the available talent pool
- *Knowing how*: The technical and collaborative skills needed to perform, enhanced by cross-functional (disciplinary) training
- *Knowing what*: Learn about your industry (not just occupation or job) and interindustry mobility by understanding the requirements for entry, opportunities, and potential threats (changing technology, obsolescence, or uncertainty)
- *Knowing where*: Gain confidence by knowing entry points, where to pursue training/learning opportunities, gain experiences
- *Knowing when*: Timing of roles, activities so that can move quickly or be willing to change perspective; will be determined by individual's choices

A skills and competencies deficit is not the only concern of employers about today's young talent. Employer representatives and management question the work behaviors and attitudes of college students and recent graduates with anecdotal stories of the attitudinal deficiencies of young adults in the workplace. For example, in a Boise State University–sponsored case study (2013), employers identified a group of behaviors, attitudes, and values that were critical for new hires to display to ensure early success in their organizations. The list included:

- Responsible and accountable for work and behavior
- Strong work ethic
- Maturity (displays sound judgment and controls emotions)
- Self-directed
- Humility
- Adaptable
- Punctual
- Professional demeanor
- Curiosity

Duckworth (2016) emphasizes that mindset (e.g., attitudes and behaviors) is especially important for superior performance. She characterizes *grit* as a combination of passion and perseverance, and continually competing with your former self to get to higher and higher performance over time. As a T-professional engages in assignments that cross multiple boundaries with diverse teams, attitudes and behaviors become critical for personal and organizational success. Concerned that the early T-models failed to capture the importance of attitudes and behaviors prompted Michigan State University scholars working on the T to insert the ME component at the intersection of the vertical and horizontal dimensions. The role of the ME provides the glue that holds the components of the T together, emphasizing the necessary possession of attitudinal capital.

Why a T-model Is Essential

In Estry and Gardner's work (2017), they cast the T-professional as an organizing principle, a vision or framework that embraces efforts to create a strong liberally educated college graduate and nimble professional. The model brings together years of work by organizations such as the Collegiate Employment Research Institute (CERI) and the Association of American Colleges & Universities (AAC&U), transforming the conversation on the importance of a liberal education and fostered the implementation of learning outcomes. The T-model validates extensive research on the critical importance of deep disciplinary knowledge and extends that thinking to encompass the significance of knowledge and interaction within and across disciplinary domains. The T-model highlights why the essential professional abilities delineated in the generally accepted goals for a liberal education are essential to student professional success.

The T-model adds two components that expand the conversation on the role of postsecondary education. First, it stresses the importance of developing a deeper knowledge of the systems, skills, and abilities needed to work within and across disciplines. Virtually no problem can be solved without crossing disciplinary boundaries, whether found in a single system or across diverse domains. Second—and the most important— the T-model focuses on the ME (the individual), discussed in detail in Chapter 4.

The T-model frames the essential components of a rigorous postsecondary education, highlighting the knowledge, attitudes, and abilities that must lie at the core of a 21st century learning experience. It helps students develop the skills to survive and thrive in a complex and challenging world where adaptive innovation and boundary spanning are the keys to success.

Critically, the T points us toward a fundamental truth about how institutions should function if they intend to foster adaptive innovation and boundary spanning advances, strive to address complex global problems, and educate the next generation of professionals. The T is the definition of student success! Although simple in theory, this model in practice requires significant cultural shifts as we determine what constitutes the learning experiences needed to develop the breadth of abilities characterized by the T. It requires top-down, bottom-up, and inter- and intra-institutional thinking along with fundamental philosophical and structural changes in the way we work and engage with others inside and outside our areas of expertise to solve problems.

References

Arthor, W. B. (2014). *Complexity and the economy*. Oxford: Oxford University Press.

Boise State University. (2013). *Employer feedback on talent needs and preparedness*. Career Services. Boise: Boise State University.

Brent, K. F., Gupta, A., & Sommer, D. (2013). *Maverick* research: surviving the rise of 'smart machines,' the loss of 'dream jobs' and '90% unemployment'*. Stamford, CT: Gartner Inc.

Briggs, J., & Peat, F. D. (1989). *Turbulent mirror: An illustrated guide to chaos theory and the science of wholeness*. New York, NY: Harper & Row.

Brown, T. (2005, June). Strategy by design. *Fast Company*. Retrieved from https://fastcompany.com/52795/strategy-design

Brown, T. (2009). *Change by design: How design thinking transforms organizations and inspires innovation*. New York, NY: Harper Business

Brown, T. (2010). *IDEO CEO Tim Brown: T-Shaped stars: The Backbone of IDEO's Collaborative Culture*. Retrieved from http://tsummit.org/http://chiefexecutive.net/ideo-ceo-tim-brown-t-shaped-stars-thebackbone-of-ideoae%E2%84%A2s-collaborative-culture/

Brynjolfsson, E., & McAfee, A. (2012). *Race against the machine: How the digital revolution is accelerating innovation, driving productivity, and irreversibly transforming employment and the economy*. Lexington, MA: Digital Frontier Press.

Brynjolfsson, E., & McAfee, A. (2014). *The second machine age: Work, progress, and prosperity in a time of brilliant technologies*. New York, NY: W.W. Norton and Company.

Chesbrough, H., & Spohrer, J. (2006). A research manifesto for service science. *Communications of ACM, 49*(7), 35–40.

Donofrio, N. (2016). *Nick Donofrio on T-shaped professionals*. Video message at the T Summit 2016 at National Academy of Sciences building: Washington DC, March 21–22, 2016. Retrieved from https://youtube.com/watch?v=EMgPCW4mlVA

Donofrio, N., Sanchez, C., & Spohrer, J. (2010). Collaborative innovation and service systems. In D. Grasso & M. B. Burkins (Eds.). *Holistic engineering education*. New York, NY: Springer.

Duckworth, A. (2016). *Grit: The power of passion and perseverance*. New York, NY: Scribner.

Employment Research Institute at Michigan State University. Retrieved from http://ceri.msu.edu/wp-content/uploads/2010/01/skillsbrief1-2010.pdf

Estry, D., & Gardner, P. (2017). A primer on the T-professional. Michigan State University: Collegiate Employment Research Institute. Retrieved from http://ceri.msu.edu/wp-content/uploads/2018/03/Primer-on-the-T-professional.pdf

Ford, M. (2015). Rise of the robots: Technology and the threat of a jobless future. New York, NY: Basic Books.

Friedman, T. L. (2016). Thank you for being late: An optimist's guide to thriving in the age of accelerations. New York, NY: Farrar, Strauss and Girous.

Gada, K. (2016). The ATOM: The Accelerating TechnOnomic Medium. Retrieved from http://atom.singularity2050.com/2016/06/executive-summary.html

Guest, D. (1991, September). The hunt is on for the renaissance man of computing. The Independent (London).

Hanneman, L., & Gardner, P. (2010). Under the economic turmoil a skill gap simmers. Michigan State University: Collegiate Employment Research Institute. Retrieved from http://ceri.msu.edu/wp-content/uploads/2010/01/skillsabrief1-2010.pdf

Hill, S. (2015). Raw deal: How the "Uber Economy" and runaway capitalism are screwing American workers. New York, NY: St. Martin's Press.

IfM, IBM. (2008). Succeeding through service innovation: A service perspective for education, research, business, and government. Cambridge: University of Cambridge Institute for Manufacturing.

Johnson, S. (2015). How we got to now: Six innovations that made the modern world. New York, NY: Riverhead Books.

Jones, C., & DeFillippi, R. J. (1996). Back to the future in film: Combining industry and self-knowledge to meet the career challenges of the 21st century. Academy of Management Perspectives, 10(4), 89–103.

Katz, L. F., & Margo, R. A. (2014). Technical change and the relative demand for skilled labor: The United States in historical perspective. In Human capital in history: The American record (pp. 15–57). Chicago, IL: University of Chicago Press.

Kauffman, S. (1996). At home in the universe: The search for laws of self-organization and complexity. Oxford, England: Oxford University Press.

Kelley, R., & Caplan, J. (1993, July/August). How bell labs creates star performers. Harvard Business Review, pp. 128–139.

Kelly, J. E., & Hamm, S. (2015). Smart machines: IBM's Watson and the era of cognitive computing. New York, NY: Columbia University Press.

Kurzweil, R. (1990). The age of the intelligent machine. Cambridge, MA: MIT Press.

Kurzweil, R. (2005). Singularity is near. New York, NY: Penguin Group.

Maglio, P. P., & Spohrer, J. (2008). Fundamentals of service science. Journal of the Academy of Marketing Science, 36(1), 18–20.

Maglio, P. P., Kieliszewski, C.A., & Spohrer, J. C. (2010). Handbook of service science. New York, NY: Springer.

March, J.G. (1991). Exploration and exploitation in organizational learning. Organizational Science, 2(1), 71–87.

Mindell, D. A. (2015). Our robots, ourselves: robotics and the myths of autonomy. New York, NY: Viking.

Moghaddam, Y., Bess, C., Demirkan, H., & Spohrer, J. (2016). T-shaped: The new breed of IT professional. Agile Product Management & Software Engineering Excellence Executive Update. Retrieved form https://cutter.com/sites/default/files/APM/apmu1608.pdf

Moghaddam, Y., Demirkan, H., & Spohrer, J. (2018). T-shaped professionals: Adaptive innovators. Service systems and innovations in business and society collection. New York, NY: Business Expert Press.

Pryor, R., & Bright, J. (2011). The chaos theory of careers: A new perspective on working in the twenty-first century. New York, NY: Routledge.

Rouse, W., & Spohrer, J. (2018). Automating versus augmenting intelligence. Journal of Enterprise Transformation. Taylor & Francis. Retrieved form https://tandfonline.com/doi/abs/10.1080/19488289.2018.1424059

Schlossberg, N. K. (1984). Counseling adults in transition: Linking practice with theory. New York, NY: Springer Publishing Company, Inc.

United States. Secretary's Commission on Achieving Necessary Skills. (1991). What work requires of schools: a SCANS report for America. Washington: U.S. Department of Education. Retrieved from https://www2.ed.gov/pubs/NatAtRisk/risk.html

Vygotcky, L. (1978). Interaction between learning and development. In Gauvain & Coles (eds). Readings on the development of children.(pp 34-40). New York: Scientific American Book.

Waldrop, M. M. (1992). Complexity: The emerging science at the edge of order and chaos. Oxford, England: Oxford University Press.

Webb, A. (2019). The big nine: How the tech titans & their thinking machines could warp humanity. New York, NY: Public Affairs.

Zone of Proximal Development. Retrieved from https://en.wikipedia.org/wiki/Zone_of_proximal_ development

Contributed Author

Philip Gardner, Ph.D., leads the Collegiate Employment Research Institute at Michigan State University. For 34 years, the institute has pursued research focused on the transition from college to work, early socialization in the workplace, national labor market trends from new college graduates, and experiential education (specifically internships and cooperative education). Phil initiated work on the T-model 10 years ago and is a strong advocate for the model as a means to reimagine undergraduate education. His collaboration with Jim Spohrer at IBM and Doug Estry at MSU has advanced our conceptualization and practice of the T-model and brought a wider understanding through three T-summits. He served as a Fulbright Specialist to New Zealand in work-integrated learning; recognized by the Cooperative Education and Internship Association and the World Association of Cooperative Education for his research in understanding and leadership in advancing work-integrated learning. He was recently elected to the Academy of Fellows of the National Association of Colleges and Employers.

Jim Spohrer directs IBM's open source Artificial Intelligence (AI) efforts in IBM's Open Technologies Group with a focus on open source developer and data science ecosystems. Previously at IBM, he led Global University Programs, co-founded Almaden Service Research, and was CTO of the Venture Capital Group. After his MIT B.S. in physics, he developed speech recognition systems at Verbex, an Exxon company, before receiving his Yale Ph.D. in Computer Science/Artificial Intelligence. In the 1990s, he attained Apple Computers' Distinguished Engineer Scientist and Technology title for next generation learning platforms. With over 90 publications and nine patents, he won the Gummesson Service Research award, Vargo and Lusch Service-Dominant Logic award, Daniel Berg Service Systems award, and a PICMET Fellow for advancing service science.

PART I

CHAPTER 1

Disciplinary, Deep Disciplinary, and Interdisciplinary Knowledge: The Stem of the T

Douglas W. Estry

The T-professional integrates depth, defined in terms of disciplinary knowledge and the ability to understand how individuals with that knowledge function and interact to accomplish a desired outcome within or across a system(s), and breadth, defined as the professional abilities that allow someone with deep disciplinary knowledge to engage meaningfully with others who possess different disciplinary knowledge in order to affect an outcome that might not otherwise be possible (Gardner and Estry 2017). The T draws on existing scholarly work that (1) underscores the importance of deep disciplinary knowledge; (2) emphasizes professional abilities essential to success in a rapidly changing digital, knowledge-based global community; (3) stresses the importance of systems thinking and deep disciplinary knowledge as an essential foundation for boundary-spanning abilities; and (4) highlights the importance of understanding self as the ability to articulate what the individual wants to accomplish (purpose), comprehend how that fits in the world (awareness), and reach outside of themselves to act (confidence). The T affirms the need for collaborative learning opportunities that foster a student's ability to understand the complexities of working within and across the boundaries of disciplines and systems while acting on and maintaining a set of core values inclusive of integrity, empathy, and a commitment to excellence.

While the T-model lacks a common language, it is understood across the diverse disciplines it is designed to connect. Establishing this language requires time and places to foster mutual understanding by spanning differences, discussing ideas, and building common meaning (Gorman 2011). Gorman refers to these as *trading zones*, or places to exchange ideas, knowledge, and negotiate compromises, all challenging pieces of bridging differences in ways of knowing and creating a common understanding and a new paradigm.

Disciplinary Knowledge

Mastery of a discipline requires the acquisition of a body of knowledge commonly used to define a specific field of study in higher education inclusive of the attitudes, abilities, ways of knowing and communicating knowledge, and attributes of an expert in a disciplinary field. The breadth and depth of disciplinary knowledge is subject to change as new knowledge is generated, often as an outcome of research and the need to address challenging new problems, problems frequently occurring at the intersection of two or more existing disciplines. These changes are inclusive of new terminology, the establishment of shared meaning, and alternative ways of communicating new ideas occasionally leading to new subdisciplines or newly defined areas of disciplinary study.

The breadth and depth of knowledge defining a discipline is determined by individuals considered experts in the field. Therefore, mastery of a disciplinary body of knowledge is essential to effective practice. This process inevitably yields implications for curriculum design (what must be taught and learned) and the assessment of that learning (what learners must know and be able to do). No matter the degree of specificity, articulation of a disciplinary body of knowledge inevitably positions prerequisite learning as an essential component.

An important goal of a discipline is to frame professional responsibility and characterize both foundational knowledge and discipline-specific content knowledge essential to professional practice (Eraut 1994; Newman, Sime, and Corcoran-Perry 1991; Blais, Hayes, Kozier, and Erb 2015; Streveler et al. 2006). Hill, Rowan, and Ball (2005), in their work on disciplinary knowledge on mathematics education, refer to this as *common knowledge of content* recognizing, as first laid out by Shulman (1986), that more than knowledge of mathematics was important to supporting mathematics learning. Mansilla (2005) noted, "A student begins to exhibit disciplinary understanding when he or she has mastered a certain disciplinary content base (for example, being able to move flexibly among theories, examples, concepts, and findings stemming from disciplinary practice)" (p. 19). Mansilla's observation aligns with the ability to apply higher order thinking skills as characterized by Bloom et al. (1956) and expanded by Airasian et al. (2001) recognizing that knowledge is inclusive of factual, conceptual, procedural, and metacognitive abilities. Again, focusing on mathematics education, Ferrini-Mundy, Floden, and McCrory (2005) defined disciplinary core content knowledge for teaching algebra as "the main ideas and concepts of the domain, the commonly applied algorithms or procedures, the organizing structures and frameworks that undergird the mathematical domain" (p. 25).

In the context of the T, core content knowledge of the discipline references an individual's understanding of foundational ideas and concepts as well as how their interrelatedness forms the larger professional body of knowledge and how this shapes professional interactions within the discipline. Specialized disciplinary knowledge often refers to the main ideas and concepts that are central to subdisciplines (e.g., biomedical or chemical engineering as a subdiscipline of engineering).

Deep Disciplinary Learning

Deep learning is a construct that reflects the learners' ability to remember, understand, and apply disciplinary concepts using this knowledge to analyze data, think critically, and develop new hypotheses. Deep disciplinary learning goes beyond a set of accumulated facts to encompass the ability to apply disciplinary concepts and ways of knowing, as well how this knowledge is produced, communicated, and used. It is evidenced by:

1. demonstrating the capacity to gather, analyze, synthesize, and communicate data;
2. seeking new meaning;
3. reflecting on learning; and
4. creating new disciplinary knowledge and concepts.

Mansilla (2005) sees this as being able to draw on disciplinary knowledge and ways of knowing (as opposed to using *naive or commonsense* explanations) as a critical hallmark of both deep disciplinary knowledge as well as the capacity to work across disciplines. The learner is able to develop, validate, alter, or dismiss existing models based on evidence. It requires active listening, understanding, and considering the perspective of others (empathy) in and outside the discipline. Deep disciplinary learning facilitates communication across disciplinary and system boundaries as well as appreciating and acting on the value and application of diverse ways of knowing and generating new conceptual knowledge to propose and implement innovative and creative new solutions.

The body of knowledge defined to encompass a discipline is more than simply an accumulated set of facts. Deep knowledge embodies a unique set of ideas about what it means to know something, and how that knowledge is produced, communicated, and used. For example, in science, technology, engineering, and math (STEM) fields, the *scientific method* is the established way of understanding the natural world. It is based on empirical observations grounded in facts, laws, and theories, and driven by a hypothesis. Other bodies of knowledge have identified ways of knowing grounded in lived experiences, observation, faith, or philosophic reasoning. We use the term *disciplinary ways of knowing* to refer to these discipline-specific sets of ideas.

In response to growing concern that the knowledge, attitudes, and abilities of recent graduates was not keeping pace with twenty-first-century demands (Association of American Colleges and Universities 2005, 2007, 2008; Gardner 1998, 2011, 2013), Kereluik, Mishra, Fahnoe, and Terry (2013) reviewed 15 seminal works focused on 21st century learning to determine if, in comparison to 20th century expectations, the framework of undergraduate knowledge had changed. Their synthesis resulted in a model for learning that consisted of three broad categories each with three subcategories. These included: (1) foundational knowledge (to know) inclusive of digital/information and communications technology (ICT) literacy, core content knowledge, and cross-disciplinary knowledge; (2) meta-knowledge (to act) inclusive of creativity and innovation, problem-solving and critical thinking, and communication and collaboration; (3) humanistic knowledge (to value) inclusive of life/job skills, ethical/emotional awareness, and cultural competence (Kereluik et al. 2013).

Combined with what has traditionally been referred to as general education, liberal education, or the integrative studies component of a college curriculum, preparing students with disciplinary knowledge has long been the mainstay of a postsecondary education. The question is whether this classic conceptualization of a curriculum meets the demands of a 21st century education. The analysis of Kereluik et al. (2013) might suggest that little has changed regarding our expectations for college graduates. However, they argue that when placed in the context of a global society and economy, the increasing pace of technological change, and the digital revolution, much has changed. In addition, there is a growing number of complex global challenges that must be addressed. These challenges compel our educational system and employers to ask whether or not we are truly teaching in innovative ways that prepares future generations with the depth of knowledge, attitudes, and abilities needed to generate creative solutions.

Postsecondary education alone does not have the capacity to independently achieve the desired deep disciplinary outcome. Collaborations among postsecondary educators and employers are needed to promote new understandings and ways of communicating, allowing for development of deep disciplinary learning. In addition, educators must continue to conceive and implement alternate ways of guiding the learning process, placing active student engagement at the core. Our collective educational responsibility cannot be either/or. Core content knowledge, no matter how critical, cannot be the focus at the expense of what Kereluik et al. (2013) refer to as *meta-knowledge* and *humanistic knowledge*.

Multi- and Interdisciplinary Learning

Considerable literature focuses on characterizing the concepts of multi-, inter-, and transdisciplinary. Despite this, there remains a lack of clarity regarding what differentiates each as it pertains to creating and assessing learning opportunities that foster the development of cross-disciplinary abilities. Rather than add to this rich array of literature,

Table 1.1 draws on the work of Mansilla (2005) and Park and Son (2010) who differentiated modes of teaching to achieve the desired cross-disciplinary learning. Relative to the characteristic disciplinary involvement, the terms *comprised of* and *drawn from* were used to signal a different type of interaction. This becomes apparent when examining the level of integration, interactions and, in particular, outcomes. What is clear is that disciplinary knowledge encompasses the knowledge, attitudes, and abilities that are characteristics of deep disciplinary learning and is therefore an essential component of either multi- or interdisciplinary engagement.

Two challenges arise when focusing on the development of interdisciplinary abilities and understanding the degree to which the goal of interdisciplinary learning can be reached through learning experience. First, Park and Son (2010) argue that the learning experiences created to develop interdisciplinary abilities have often been designed and analyzed using multidisciplinary expectations. They lay out five learning modes, each

Table 1.1 Characteristics of multi- vs. interdisciplinary learning

Defining Characteristics	Multidisciplinary	Interdisciplinary
Discipline involvement	Comprised of two or more disciplines	Drawn from two or more disciplines
Disciplinary knowledge	Requires deep disciplinary knowledge	Requires deep disciplinary knowledge
Integration	Not fully integrated, superficial merging of viewpoints and disciplinary concepts	Fully integrated—builds on and extends disciplinary knowledge, concepts, ways of knowing
Interactions	Characterized by disciplinary independence, sharing and learning from other disciplines occurs but work is primarily within disciplinary boundaries using disciplinary concepts	Characterized by interdependence, collaboration, negotiation, compromise based on a shared understanding and application of language and conceptual frameworks
Outcomes	Results are primarily grounded in disciplinary knowledge, concepts, and ways of knowing	Results generate new and/or expanded knowledge, concepts, and an integration of ways of knowing that are shared across disciplinary boundaries

(Mansilla 2005; Park and Son 2010)

requiring a different way of engaging the students and each requiring the student and teacher to assume different roles. At the level of inter/trans-disciplinary, they note in that the type of interactivity is focused on *learner collaboration and participation* with the intent that it is *new knowledge creation driven* with the student assuming the identity of *knowledge collaborator and producer* and the teacher's identity as an *interactive learning designer* (Table 1.1, p. 85). Second, Mansilla (2015) argues that an assessment keyed to expectations for the outcomes of interdisciplinary learning is critical. She proposes three components (p. 18) of a rubric that could be used to determine the degree to which learners are demonstrating interdisciplinary:

- Is the work grounded in carefully selected and adequately employed disciplinary insights?
- Are disciplinary insights clearly integrated to leverage student understanding?
- Does the work exhibit a clear sense of purpose, reflectivity, and self-critique?

The T-model is closely associated with the process of design thinking used to successfully create innovative solutions to complex problems by understanding a problem from the perspectives of multiple stakeholders as viewed through the eyes of interdisciplinary teams. Philip Gardner (personal communication), Director of the Collegiate Employment Research Institute, provides an example from a project focused on economic development in Thailand where he led a team comprised of a water engineer, salt-tolerant crop specialist, and labor utilization specialist all focused on developing models for conversion of underutilized land into productive farms. These disciplinary experts had to create a shared language in order to communicate effectively, understand alternative perspectives, and expand or enhance understanding of disciplines different from their own. This shared language allowed specialists to gain mutual understanding of their respective areas and the value associated with different ways of knowing. This example illustrates the value of inter-disciplinary engagement used to generate new knowledge, alternative solutions, new conceptual ideas, and new applications through applying knowledge and skills that bridge both disciplines and systems, developing solutions that might not otherwise have been possible.

Engaging with others trained in disparate disciplines goes beyond the transfer of knowledge. While disciplinary language may be a barrier that needs to be addressed, it becomes more about the way we think in interdisciplinary situations—our mindset, acceptance of different ways of knowing, empathy, willingness to suspend judgment, curiosity, and perseverance until a solution is found. How does the economist, the water engineer, the crop scientist, and the community development specialist work together? First, they must be open-minded and willing to explore a problem from various perspectives, something Strober (2011) says is a major stumbling block. She also believes they need patience, "suspending judgment until they obtain some mastery of strange ideas and methods" (p. 4). Strober's (2011) work would suggest that although deep disciplinary knowledge remains a critical piece of effective interdisciplinary work, thoughtfully constructed interdisciplinary learning opportunities during the formative periods in postsecondary education could lower barriers to effective collaboration by establishing interdisciplinary thinking as a common component of all disciplinary ways of knowing.

Intentional and unintentional interdisciplinary environments emerge across most campuses in various forms. To advance T-principles, institutions need to creatively develop and intentionally promote these interdisciplinary environments. The ensuing interdisciplinary conversations will allow students to suspend their models, personal judgments, and biases and work toward understanding alternative perspectives. These experiences will impart confidence to traverse disciplinary boundaries and recognize that boundary-spanning competencies applied across disciplines and systems often lead to more comprehensive solutions to complex problems.

Deep disciplinary knowledge is core to the functioning of a T-professional. Traditionally, postsecondary education fosters disciplinary content knowledge inclusive of concepts, theories, and applications. However, the issue is the degree to which traditional models of undergraduate learning keep pace with the increasing rate of change particularly related to technological innovations and the complexity, global nature, and diversity of challenges that can only be addressed through interdisciplinary collaborations. As Kereluik et al. (2013) point out, first we need to understand what a 21st century learning experience is. We then must recognize that creating learning experiences that foster deep disciplinary knowledge and interdisciplinary abilities is a complex systems problem requiring the development of *trading zones* (Gorman 2011) in which creative new approaches to enhancing students' didactic and professional abilities are conceived. This is not either a postsecondary or corporate sector problem. It is a both/and problem that requires T-professionals coming together to develop new and creative solutions to a life-long learning experience.

References

Airasian, P. W., Cruikshank, K. A., Mayer, R. E., Pintrich, P. R., Raths, J., & Wittrock, M. C. (2001). In L. W. Anderson & D. R. Krathwohl (Eds.), *A taxonomy for learning, teaching, and assessing: A revision of bloom's taxonomy of educational objectives* (complete edition). New York, NY: Longman.

Association of American Colleges & Universities. (2005). *Liberal education outcomes: A preliminary report on student achievement in college.* Washington DC: Association of American Colleges & Universities. Retrieve from https://aacu.org/sites/default/files/files/LEAP/LEAP_Report_2005.pdf

Association of American Colleges & Universities. (2007). *College learning for the new global century: A report from the national leadership council for liberal education & America's promise. Washington* DC: Association of American Colleges & Universities.

Association of American Colleges & Universities. (2008). *High-impact educational practices: What they are, who has access to them, and why they matter.* Washington DC: Association of American Colleges & Universities.

Blais, K., Hayes, J. S., Kozier, B., & Erb, G. L. (2015). *Professional nursing practice: Concept and perspectives (7th ed.).* Hoboken, NJ: Prentice Hall.

Bloom, B. S., Engelhart, M. D., Furst, E. J., Hill, W. H., & Krathwohl, D. R. (1956). *Taxonomy of educational objectives: The classification of educational goals. Handbook I: Cognitive domain.* New York, NY: David McKay Company.

Eraut, M. (1994). *Developing professional knowledge and competence.* Abingdon, U.K. Routledge/Psychology Press.

Ferrini-Mundy, J., Floden, R., & McCrory, R. (2005). *Knowledge for Teaching School Algebra: Challenges in Developing An Analytics Framework.* Retrieved From https://msu.edu/user/mccrory/pubs/Ferrini_KATFramewokr.pdf

Gardner, P. (1998). Are seniors ready to work? In J. N. Gardner & G. Van der Veer. *The senior year experience: Facilitating integration, reflection, closure, and transition.* San Francisco, CA: Jossey-Bass.

Gardner, P. (2011). *CERI Thought Piece: Internships As High Stakes Events.* Retrieved From http://ceri.msu.edu/wp-content/uploads/2010/01/High-Stakes-Internships.pdf

Gardner, P. (2013). Framing internships from an employer perspective: Length, number and relevance. *CERI Research Brief 6-2013.* Retrieved From http://ceri.msu.edu/wp-content/up-loads/2010/01/internshipCERI-Research-Brief-XX.pdf

Gardner, P., & Estry, D. (2017). *A primer on the T-professional.* Michigan: Collegiate Employment Research Institute, Michigan State University.

Gorman, M. E. (2011). *Trading zones and interactional expertise: Creating new kinds of collaboration.* Cambridge, MA: MIT Press.

Hill, H. C., Rowan, B., & Ball, D. L. (2005). Effects of teachers' mathematical knowledge for teaching on student achievement. *America Educational Research Journal, 42*(2), 371–406.

Kereluik, K., Mishra, P., Fahnoe, C., & Terry, L. (2013). What knowledge is of most worth. *Journal of Digital Learning in Teacher Education, 29*(4), 127–140.

Mansilla, V. B. (2005). Assessing student work at disciplinary crossroads. *Change, 37*(1), 14–21.

Newman, M. A., Sime, A. M., & Corcoran-Perry, S. A. (1991). The focus of the discipline of nursing. *Advances in Nursing Science, 14*(1), 1–6.

Park, J., Son, J. (2010). Transitioning toward transdisciplinary learning in a multidisciplinary environment. *International Journal of Pedagogies and Learning, 6*(1), 82–93.

Shulman, L. S. (1986). Those who understand: knowledge growth in teaching. *Educational Researcher,* 15, 4–14.

Streveler, R. A., Geist, M. R., Ammerman. R. F., Sulzbach, C. S., Miller, R. L., Olds, B. M., & Nelson, M. A. (2006). *The development of a professional knowledge base: The persistence of substance-based schemas in engineering students.* In Annual Meeting of the American Educational Research Association.

Strober, M. H. (2011). *Interdisciplinary conversations: Challenging habits of thought.* Stanford, CA: Stanford University Press.

Texley, J. (2007, Winter). Twenty-first century skills for tomorrow's leaders. *Peer Review, 9*(1). Washington, DC: Association of American Colleges & Universities. Retrieved from https://aacu.org/publications-research/periodicals/twenty-first-century-skills-tomorrow's-leaders

Contributed Author

Doug Estry, PhD., served as Associate Provost for Undergraduate Education and Dean of Undergraduate Studies at Michigan State University. In this role he was responsible for overseeing university-level undergraduate initiatives that support and enhance the undergraduate learning experience. He also served as Graduate Director and subsequently Program Director of the BLD Program and as the Associate Dean for Student and Academic Affairs in the College of Natural Science. During his tenure as Associate Dean, he focused on the issues of teaching and learning in science and mathematics including work to advance a culture of learning outcomes assessment.

CHAPTER 2

Deep Systems Knowledge Brings System Thinking

Philip Gardner and Heather Maietta

Introduction

The Secretary's Commission on Achieving Necessary Skills (SCANS) (1991) report set forth the necessity that workers understand, not only their own work role, but their actions in the context of the work of the others around them. This internal perspective positioned each employee as a member of an organizational system where they were expected to understand the different parts of the system and their connections as outlined into three "elements": *functional skills* or an understanding of what people actually do at work; *enabling skills* or specific knowledge and procedures developed through educational means; and *scenario* or the ability to demonstrate the way in which work integrates these skills into workplace outcomes. By monitoring one's own performance, workers could anticipate consequences to their actions, identify emerging trends, recognize problems in the system, and integrate *multiple displays of data* (Kane, Berryman, Goslin, and Meltzer 1990). Systems and a systems way of thinking as a desired skill set essentially remained dormant until Jim Spohrer, IBM's Director of Cognitive OpenTech and colleague's research on service science, thrust system thinking again into the forefront (Maglio and Spohrer 2008; Spohrer, Golinelli, Piciocchi, and Bassano 2010). Systems thinking has been a central component of IBM's Service Science and Smarter Planet initiatives since their beginning (Spohrer and Maglio 2009).

IBM's contribution strengthened the earliest T-model by inserting systems knowledge as a depth component (Donofrio et al. 2010). During the company's pursuit of solutions to key societal issues, they came to realize that solving a problem from a disciplinary approach (engineering, computer science, chemistry, or economics) may resolve the problem from one discipline's perspective only to have the problem rear-up in another place in the system for another discipline to solve (Spohrer et al. 2012). In essence, the problem was not completely resolved. In Gardner's (2009) *5 Minds for the Future*, he outlines that individuals do need to be experts in at least one area or "discipline," yet, also able to assemble information from disparate sources, apply creativity, exercise diverse thought and adaptability, and apply these attributes through an ethical lens. IBM recognized that their teams needed to approach a problem from a systems perspective to ensure the final solution did not merely manifest larger problems elsewhere. Awareness of systems knowledge is common throughout the literature on problem solving, but IBM stressed that their employees demonstrate a deep understanding of system knowledge and the application of that knowledge to create viable solutions to pressing service problems.

Systems Framework

An initial task of this chapter is to establish an agreed upon yet simple definition of a system. From the dictionary, systems are "a group of related parts that move or work together" or "a group of devices or artificial objects or an organization forming a network especially for distributing something or serving a common purpose" (Merriam-Webster 2013). Yet, Meadows (2008) addresses a system's basic principle as "something more than the sum of its parts" (p.188) or more specifically as a set of parts, elements, or entities that are *coherently organized*, interconnected, and interdependent, whose structure serves a function or purpose based on the result of a series of actions or a set of behaviors.

An organized system is comprised of building blocks or components. Meadows (2008) identifies three components that every system contains: elements, interconnections, and a function or purpose. The majority of the systems elements are easily recognized because they can be seen, having tangible parts, pieces, or equipment. However, some elements are not readily seen but are essential, such as information that drives the system, attitudes, and behaviors.

Interconnections, or the relations between the elements, is what holds the system together by sending messages (signals) between the parts. Knowledge of all the system relationships is incomplete, suggesting that interconnections are less understood than system elements (Meadows 2008). Interconnections are represented in systems by flows—either physical flows such as money, standards, content knowledge or nonphysical flows of information, informal knowledge, or ideas. Incomplete information leads to a potential problem as actions fail to materialize unless information on resources, incentives, and consequences are also available (Meadows 2008).

Meadows (2008) indicates that the hardest component to understand is the system's function or purpose. "A system's function or purpose is not necessarily spoken, written, or expressed explicitly, except through the operation of the system. The best way to deduce the system's purpose is to watch for a while to see how the system behaves" (p. 14). Several useful terms guide our understanding of systems:

- *Stocks*: Stocks are the elements of the system that can be felt, counted, measured, or seen at any time (Meadows 2008). Includes stored information collected through the system that increases the *complexity of the mechanism* (Margalef 1963, 1969).
- *Flows*: Flows are change of stocks over time (in and out of the system).
- *Dynamics*: Dynamics are the behavior of the system or any component over time, which increases complexity.
- *Feedback loops*: Feedback loops are formed when changes in the stock occur that affect the flows in or out of the stock or how the system operates (Meadows 2008). Some feedback loops are simple and have a direct influence on the system, but others can be more complex, involving time lags or encountering buffers, which can either reinforce or destabilize stocks.

When addressing complex problems, individuals or project teams must understand the system in which the problem lies. This requires the use of systems thinking to understand the depth of "the complex behavior in order to better predict them and, ultimately, adjust their outcomes" (Arnold and Wade 2015, p. 670). Thus, systems thinking can be described as the weaving together of three modes of thought: (1) *induction* to generate possible rules and generalities from distinct observations and experiences; (2) *abduction* to compare those rules and generalities across different systems; and (3) *deduction* to apply those to specific occurrences (Hurst 2013). In terms of the T-model, systems thinking is depicted in the horizontal stroke across the top of the T.

Demands of Systems Thinking

Arnold and Wade (2015) surveyed the different definitions of system thinking since the terms were introduced by Barry Richmond in 1987. They then critiqued these definitions against a systems framework adapted from Meadows (2008) that consists of three components: *elements* (characteristics), *interconnections*, and a *function* or purpose (Arnold and Wade 2015). All existing definitions failed the test against this framework. They then developed their own definition of system thinking, which fits nicely within the construct of the T-model. In developing their definition, they recognized that "systems thinking could be viewed as a system. Systems thinking is, literally, a system of thinking about systems" (p. 670). Arnold and Wade (2015) offer an objective definition of system thinking (in other words, this definition has an expressed function or purpose): "Systems thinking is a set of synergistic analytical skills used to improve the capability of identifying and understanding systems, predicting their behaviors, and devising modification to them in order to produce desired effects" (p. 675). These skills work together as a system and include the following elements as defined by Arnold and Wade (2015):

- Systems: Groups or combinations of interrelated, interdependent, or interacting elements forming collective entities.

- Synergistic: Characteristic of synergy, which is the interaction of elements in a way that, when combined, produce a total effect that is greater than the sum of the individual elements.
- Analytical skills: Skills that provide the ability to visualize, articulate, and solve both complex and uncomplicated problems and concepts and make decisions that are sensible and based on available information. Such skills include demonstration of the ability to apply logical thinking to gathering and analyzing information, designing and testing solutions to problems, and formulating plans.
- Identify: To recognize as being a particular thing.
- Understand: To be thoroughly familiar with; apprehend clearly the character, nature, or subtleties of.
- Predict: To foretell as a deducible consequence.
- Devise modifications: To contrive, plan, or elaborate changes or adjustments

Arnold and Wade (2015) addressed the elements and interconnections components, as specified by Meadows (2008), and categorized as these stocks or the resources available to a system, changes in resource or stock levels labeled as flows, and variables that they described as the "changeable parts of the system that affects resources and flows" (p. 677). Stocks, flows, and variables behave linearly, but Arnold and Wade (2015) suggest that nonlinear behaviors also occur and should be recognized separately. Arnold and Wade depict systems thinking as a "series of continuous feedback loops" (p. 676) with no function ceasing at a final node. Rather, feedback continuously improves the connected elements. As such, they lay out eight key attributes that those employing systems thinking must be vigilant (pp. 676–77):

Recognizing interconnections: This skill involves the ability to identify key connections between parts of a system.

Identifying and understanding feedback: This ability requires identifying feedback loops and understanding how they impact system behavior.

Understanding system structure: This ability centers on understanding the system's elements and their interconnections and how this structure facilitates system behavior.

Differentiating types of stocks, flows, and variables (linear): An understanding of the operational functions and an awareness of/or ability to differentiate the array of resources (supplies and services that are necessary to keep the system functioning) available in a system, how resources levels change (flow), and the variables influencing resources and flows is required.

Identifying and understanding nonlinear relationships: An ability to recognize that some resources and flows are behaving in a nonlinear fashion.

Understanding dynamic behavior: An ability to recognize the dynamic nature of a system that stems from interconnections of stocks, flows, and variables, forming feedback loops.

Reducing complexity by modeling system conceptually: An ability to reduce the complexity of a system by modeling different elements of the system that may require the use of different methods, such as reduction and abstraction, for example (Ward 2011). This process allows a system to be viewed in different ways.

Understanding system at different scales: The ability to recognize different scales of systems.

Peter Senge (2006, 1999) has spent his career examining organizational systems and the role systems thinking plays in advancing organizations. From his body of work, he elucidates six important requirements for individuals engaged in systems thinking:

1. A deep commitment to learning
2. Being prepared to be wrong or alternatively open to challenging your own mental models
3. A willingness to reshape those models
4. Possessing empathy, which is defined as the ability to listen to others and come to understand their perspective and knowledge
5. Having the ability to work as a team, effectively collaborating to address intra- and intersystem challenges
6. Exercising patience and perseverance.

This brief overview of systems does not adequately capture the deep complexity and dynamic nature of systems though Senge (1990, 2006), Arnold and Wade (2015) allude to these conditions. It should not come as a surprise in order to gain a deep understanding of a system requires a commitment of time and effort. In a discussion with Jim Spohrer, he stated "learning a system takes more effort and is more difficult than gaining mastery of a discipline" (personal communication 2019). Because of the investment necessitated in gaining deep knowledge, the placement of systems on the vertical dimension of the T-model appears strategically aligned with mastery of a discipline.

Systems thinking emerges from investment in learning a system and serves as a guide for our understanding of a system and multiple systems working together. The requirements to engage in system thinking embrace a range of abilities and attitudes that align with the horizontal (breadth) dimension of the T-model. However, by playing a dual role, systems understanding and systems thinking strengthen both the depth and breadth of the T. From this discussion, we grasp the importance of system understanding to the T. This component, combined with the ME of the T, as detailed in Chapter 4, can be considered the glue that holds the T-model together. The challenge rests on introducing systems and systems thinking more intentionally into the undergraduate learning experience. Faculty address systems from various disciplinary perspectives, but rarely is systems thinking intentionally used as an organizing principle around designing cross campus learning experiences.

Implications for Higher Education

Bringing systems as a dimension of undergraduate learning experiences will have to be approached from several directions. First, the presentation of the systems construct should be delivered in a manner that is easily understood and accepted by students, who must be able to connect their interests, goals, and aspirations to construct a curricular and cocurricular path that reflects reality. The second approach accepts that to develop T-graduates will require multiple agents, many located beyond the boundaries of the classroom and even off-campus. These approaches come with some steep challenges emanating from the mindset and organization of higher education institutions.

A practical means of introducing systems in a school or workplace setting is to frame systems around visible, everyday occurrences. This approach is exactly what Spohrer's IBM service science team did in expounding on service science theory, making service science accessible to people from all persuasions. Spohrer's team recognized that the problems they were solving tended to cluster in certain service systems that citizens encounter daily. Explaining the T-model from IBM's perspective became much easier by putting a systems lens up to the service sectors that they were addressing. For example, Spohrer operationalized the system concept around IBM's highly effective Smart Planet initiative, thus allowing those unfamiliar with more academic presentations of systems to ground this dimension in something real, something they could recognize (Spoher and Maglio 2009). Spohrer articulates the 13 system groups classified in three clusters that IBM believes each of us interacts with in our daily lives:

Systems that focus on the flow of things:

1. Transportation and supply chain
2. Water and waste recycling
3. Food and products
4. Energy and electric grid
5. Information, information and communications technology (ICT), and Cloud

Systems that focus on human activities and development

1. Building and construction
2. Retail and hospitality (including media and entertainment)
3. Banking and finance (includes business and consulting)
4. Health care and family life
5. Education and work life (including entrepreneurship)

Systems that focus on governing

1. Governing at local level
2. Governing at regional and state level
3. Governing at national level

Courses directed at systems are found on campus whether housed in specific department or as part of instruction across several disciplines. Faculty are aware of the need to study systems as Chuck Keating (Professor of Engineering Management and Systems Engineering at Old Dominion University) states: "We deal with systems in nearly every aspect of our lives and suffer the ill effects of their deficiencies" (found at https://odu.edu/cepd/engineering/systems-thinking). The challenge becomes how to escape the boundaries of the discipline and make system understanding accessible to all students.

Spohrer, in his early presentations on Service Science, offers a possible solution. He argues that the university departments can be rearranged around the 13 service areas, which are now the focal point of the institution. Faculty from each discipline are connected to at least one system through teaching, research, or service. This approach also offers connections to organizations and individuals outside the institution who operate within these systems. A student entering the institution can identify with a system seeing how the various disciplines contribute to sustaining and enhancing the system and, just as important, identify pathways for professional opportunities.

This idea is doable. In preparation of the first T-summit hosted by IBM and MSU Estry mocked up a grid of the 13 systems and cross linked to research activities on campus, courses, and university outreach activities. Each of the 13 systems were represented by at least one research activity, by multiple faculty from different disciplines involved in each system through teaching or service involvement, and by engagement of professional staff leading experiential activities. The emerging picture showed that those working in the same service area were seldom connected, preventing students from seeing the system as a system but instead as disjointed parts. Spohrer's IBM approach has a natural affinity to large research universities but smaller schools, especially liberal arts institutions, can creatively organize around a subset of systems which faculty and staff coalesce around.

Multiple actors will be necessary to pull off developing T-students. This may present challenges for higher education institutions. Initiatives for institutional advancement, particularly those related to curriculum, are the purview of the faculty. The mindset shapes around a faculty–student dyad when designing learning. However, this is no longer practical. Learning takes in multiple contexts both on and off campus. Some faculty will be directly involved but will have to accept learning experiments designed by others.

To succeed institutions will operate as a dynamic system. Many of the attempts to foster development of T-components will bubble up across campus, both in and out of the classroom. These separate endeavors should have an environment conducive to connecting their activities because they share a common purpose. Likewise, top administrators and senior faculty must signal an institutionalwide support for T-development activities, a willingness to provide resources and rewards to encourage initiatives, and strength to reduce some of the inherent problems that impede or raise barriers to educational design initiatives.

These impediments flow from the structure and organization of higher education and include the piecemeal approach to design, the failure to integrate solution ideas, the discipline-by-discipline (silos) problem-solving approach, and the incentives to stay within the existing system boundaries (Banathy 1991). These impediments run counter to the principles of the T-model, which depends on collaboration, trust, boundary spanning, and adaptive behaviors. To achieve a T-mindset, institutions must overcome these impediments or see their solutions fail to attain their promise, as Banathy indicates:

- *Incremental approach*: sends signals that you are just experimenting around the edges of the existing system. The solutions do not fit into something bigger because "no blueprint for integrating" solutions exist (Banathy 1991, p. 11). Essentially a map of the system does not exist.
- *Lack of a system orientation*: no way to integrate ideas, efforts, or resources because of an inability to make meaningful connections.
- *Staying within boundaries*: by changing only at the margins fails to recognize the complexity of T-student development nor the important interactions with any of the other of the 12 service sectors, which undermines the T's strong linkage to the workforce. As Banathy (1991) concludes, "this approach will not ensure the attainment of what is wanted" (p. 12).

The education and workforce changes that will occur over the next 20 years will consist of an entirely different set of opportunities and challenges—far greater than the ones seen by our world to date. Fluency in technology, language, and culture will be an entry-level requirement for many industries and will be sought-after by all vying for talent. Systems understanding combined with systems thinking is a critical component of the T. As the problems in society grow in complexity, it will require individuals to embrace a system mindset—the ability to recognize opportunity and then have the skills and relational ability to take advantage of this opportunity. Systems thinking provides one with the ability to think differently, breaking massive problems into smaller parts, solving those problems around systems and how systems interconnect—this is the product of the T. Without this element within the T, it will be difficult to effectively engage with problem-solving at the workplace.

References

Arnold, R. D., & Wade, J. P. (2015). A definition of systems thinking: A system approach. *Procedia Computer Science, 44*, 669–678.

Banathy, B. H. (1991). Designing social systems. *Systems science and cybernetics v. II.* pp. 1-17.

Donofrio, N., Sanchez, C., & Spohrer, J. (2010). Collaborative innovation and service systems. In D. Grasso (Ed), *Holistic engineering education* (pp. 243–269). New York, NY: Springer.

Gardner, H. (2009). *5 Minds for the future.* Cambridge, MA: Harvard Business Review Press.

Hurst, D. (2013). *T-Shaped People: Deduction, Induction, Abduction and Systems Thinking.* Retrieved from http://davidkhurst.com/t-shaped-people-deduction-induction-abduction-and-systems-thinking/

Kane, M., Berryman, S., Goslin, D., & Meltzer, A. (1990). *The secretary's commission on achieving necessary skills: Identifying and describing the skills required by work.* Washington, DC: Pelavin Associates, Inc.

Maglio, P.P. & Spohrer, J. (2008). Fundamentals of service science. *Journal of the Academy of Marketing Science, 36,* 18-20.https://doi.org/10.1007/s11747-007-0058-9

Margalef, R. (1963). On certain unifying principles in ecology. *The American Naturalist, 97*(897), 357–374.

Margalef, R. (1969). Diversity and stability: A practical proposal and a model of interdependence. *Diversity and stability in ecological systems: Brookhaven Symposia in Biology, 22,* 925–937.

Meadows, D. H. (2008). In D. Wright (Ed), *Thinking in systems: A primer.* VT: Chelsea Green Publishing.

Senge, Peter M. (1990; 2006). *The fifth discipline : the art and practice of the learning organization.* New York :Doubleday/Currency,

Spohrer, J. & Maglio, P. P. (2009). Service science: Toward a smarter planet. In Karwowski & Salvendy (Eds.), *Service Engineering.* New York, NY: Wiley.

Spohrer, J., Golinelli, G. M., Piciocchi, P., & Bassano, C. (2010). An integrated SS-VSA analysis of changing job roles. *Service Science, 2*(1–2), 1–20. Retrieved from https://doi.org/10.1007/s11747-007-0058-9

Spohrer, J., Maglio, P. P., Bailey, J. & Gruhl, D. (2007). Steps toward a science of service systems. Computer, 40(1), 71-77.

United States. Secretary's Commission on Achieving Necessary Skills. (1991). *What work requires of schools: a SCANS report for America.* Washington: U.S. Department of Education. Retrieved from https://www2.ed.gov/pubs/NatAtRisk/risk.html

Wade, J. (2011). Systems engineering: At the crossroads of complexity. In *Kongsberg systems engineering event.*

Merriam-Webster (2013). Definition of system. Retrieved from https://merriam-webster.com/dictionary/system

Contributed Author

Philip Gardner, PhD., leads the Collegiate Employment Research Institute at Michigan State University. For 34 years the Institute has pursued research focused on the transition from college to work, early socialization in the workplace, national labor market trends from new college graduates, and experiential education (specifically internships and cooperative education). Phil initiated work on the T-model 10 years ago and is a strong advocate for the model as a means to reimagine undergraduate education. His collaboration with Jim Spohrer at IBM and Doug Estry at MSU has advanced our conceptualization and practice of the T-model and brought a wider understanding through three T-summits. He served as a Fulbright Specialist to New Zealand in work-integrated learning;

recognized by the Cooperative Education and Internship Association and the World Association of Cooperative Education for his research in understanding and leadership in advancing work-integrated learning. He was recently elected to the Academy of Fellows of the National Association of Colleges and Employers.

Heather Maietta, EdD is an Associate Professor in the Doctorate of Higher Education Leadership at Regis College. Her research areas include college to workforce readiness and transition; first generation doctoral student persistence and completion; and transfer students (particularly those forced to transfer due to college closures). Heather is a Board Certified Coach who maintains a successful career and executive coaching practice careerinprogress.com where she has consulted for organizations such as Stanford, the Care New England, Johnson & Johnson, Florida International, University of Texas, 3M, Marriott, and Staples to name a few.

CHAPTER 3

Boundary Spanning and Performance: Applying Skills and Abilities Across Work Contexts

Patricia M. Rowe and Maureen T. B. Drysdale

Boundary Spanning Defined

Traditionally, managers and human resource professionals seek to hire and promote individuals who possess the knowledge, skills, and abilities (KSAs) in their discipline necessary for successful job performance. The T-model, however, argues that in addition to deep disciplinary knowledge, individuals must have the ability to interact with people with depth in different disciplines as well as those across varying organizational, political, cultural, and societal boundaries. This *boundary spanning ability* permits them to build partnerships and collaborate with others by developing sustainable relationships, managing through negotiation and influences, and seeking to understand roles, motives, and responsibilities (Williams 2002). Boundary spanning, referred to as the horizontal stroke, is unique to the T-model and thus requires further examination.

As Beechler, Søndergaard, Miller, and Bird (2004) point out, boundary spanning can be considered at the organizational or the individual level. At the organizational level, boundary spanning refers to the need for organizations to develop more flexible structures rather than to maintain traditional rigid boundaries between functions and tasks. At the individual level, boundary spanning is the set of skills and abilities that are evidenced through communication behaviors and interpersonal networks. Here we are considering boundary spanning at the individual level, though to be a boundary spanner, one must be in an organization with flexible boundaries.

What exactly are boundary spanning abilities? For the most part, these abilities have been poorly defined and are descriptions of what various authors have thought might be important. For example, one of the earliest papers by Tushman and Scanlan (1981) stated that boundary spanners are able to establish strong connections and communicate with individuals in the same internal work unit and in different external work units. Later, Williams reviewed the literature on boundary spanning abilities and categorized the articles as dealing with networking skills, innovative behavior, the ability to engage with others, engender trust, personality variables, and facilitative leadership behaviors (Williams 2002). In comparison, Miller (2008) described boundary spanning abilities as consisting of behaviors such as being able to work easily in multiple contexts, understanding the complexities of collaboration, using a wide variety of contacts, engendering trust and respect from constituents, working to unite and mobilize disparate groups, and collecting and disseminating information. Solet added the following personality traits to the above definition: alert, active, risk-taker, secure learner, flexible, emphatic, committed, curious, tolerant of ambiguity, good communicator, and humble (as cited in Wilson 2009). Additionally Strober (2011) described boundary spanners as being open-minded, willing to explore problems from various perspectives, being patient, and willing to suspend judgment. Clearly, while such an inventory of abilities and skills is interesting, it fails to be of much use in assessing whether an individual, in fact, possesses them. It is important, therefore, to define and measure this multitude of diverse skills and abilities and determine which ones distinguish between T-individuals and those who are not T's.

Relatively few systematic studies have been conducted on boundary spanning behaviors and the skills and abilities related to these behaviors. In Tushman and Scanlan's (1981) study, boundary spanning was assessed by counting the number and direction of work-related oral communications one day each week over a 15-week period. The researchers then used the data sets to designate boundary spanners and nonspanners, or in their terms, communication "stars" and "nonstars." Further analysis revealed that perceived work-related competence was positively related to the likelihood of an individual becoming a boundary spanner. In two other studies, boundary spanners were defined as professionals who were referenced by their organizational colleagues when asked who they went to for help or advice on work-related matters (Hsu, Wang, and Tzeng 2007; Sparrowe, Liden, Wayne, and Kraimer 2001). Using the answers to this question, Sparrowe and colleagues (2001) found that those who attained high scores on this question also received higher performance assessments than those with lower scores. Hsu and colleagues (2007) found that boundary spanners, as assessed by this question, were likely to be more innovative in their performance, had higher work-related competence, and higher status in the organization compared to nonboundary spanners. Additionally, Sandmann, Jordan, Mull, and Valentine (2014) developed a 32-item self-report scale, which measured, what they called, boundary spanning behaviors on four dimensions: technical-practical (I manage projects), socioemotional (I resolve conflict among other individuals), community (I communicate the community's interests to others), and organization (I develop partnerships that benefit the organization). Worth noting is that these four dimensions were found to be highly intercorrelated. Finally, Onishi (2016) developed another 30-item boundary spanning questionnaire and administered it to 4,918 nurses in Japan. Factor analysis of the responses yielded three factors: boundary spanning nurse supervisors (1) helped staff to connect and collaborate with external groups, (2) informed staff about work expectations of external groups and provided information about the team to other departments, and lastly, (3) brought knowledge from other units to solve problems. A major limitation of this study is that the effective nurse supervisors were presumed to be boundary spanners, which is a less appropriate definition in comparison to those used by other researchers.

Research on boundary spanning indicates that the success of applying skills and abilities across work contexts requires that boundary spanners have strong communication skills, are very competent, innovative, high-performing individuals, and are often (but not necessarily) of high status in the organization. Consideration of the behaviors ascribed to boundary spanners discussed to this point suggests that some of the characteristics of boundary spanners may be personality variables. Drawing upon the five-factor model of personality variables (Digman 1990), one might speculate that boundary spanners would have high scores on measures of the factors of openness to experience and conscientiousness, moderate levels of extraversion and agreeableness, and lower levels of neuroticism. While no research has been found to support such a relationship to boundary spanning, there is evidence that these five factors are related to national innovation (Steel, Rinnie, and Fairweather 2012), transformational leadership (Judge and Bono 2000), entrepreneurial success (Leutner, Ahmetoglu, Akhtar, and Chamorro-Premuzic 2014), and success in making money (Nyhus and Pons 2005).

Whether examining the descriptive behaviors or the few behaviors found in the limited research studies mentioned above, the question arises as to whether the skills necessary for these behaviors are innate or developed through experience; in other words, nature versus nurture. If boundary spanning skills, or some subset of them, are inherent characteristics of the individual, then the issue becomes one of selecting individuals with these traits and providing the appropriate environment for them to flourish. If these characteristics are largely developed through training and experience, our concern becomes one of the appropriate educational programs and subsequent training in the organization for boundary spanning abilities to thrive. Even those individuals who possess such natural abilities may benefit from opportunities to practice them in higher education, and those lacking innateness may benefit from programs that help them develop the necessary skills that compensate for those deficiencies.

Boundary Spanning, Knowledge Integration Programs, and Work-Integrated Learning

The last few decades have seen an explosion in the number of highly specialized undergraduate programs offered by colleges and universities. Incoming students are asked to select a program often without having any real idea of the content or the careers for which the program prepares them. In contrast to these specialized programs, some universities have developed very broad, interdisciplinary degree offerings across arts and science faculties with many electives and few constraints. Many of these programs purport to develop graduates who possess boundary spanning skills, though few are designed to assist the student in making connections across their courses.

One program explicitly designed to produce T-graduates is the knowledge integration program at the University of Waterloo in Canada. What makes this program different from the many interdisciplinary programs elsewhere is its core courses. As Jernigan (2018), the program's founder designed the core to consist of "a sequence of meta-skills courses explicitly developing the connections across the disciplines and equipping our students with the framework for knowing and understanding their world from multiple perspectives as well as the skills for making a difference that matters" (para. 15). From their first year in the program, students work on projects in teams made up of participants from different programs with diverse interests. These students are mentored and explicitly taught how to integrate the different perspectives of their fellow team members. By their final year, they complete a research project and integrative thesis. These core courses constitute only one-quarter of the program; another quarter consists of required courses in both arts and science faculties, and the remaining half of their program is elective, permitting students to develop more breadth or to gain depth in a particular area. Jernigan (2018) claims that graduates are effective communicators and boundary spanners who can work across disciplinary, geopolitical, socioeconomic, and ethnic boundaries. Indeed, the graduates of the program have found satisfying careers in a variety of fields and speak appreciatively of their undergraduate program.

A second program worth mentioning is work-integrated learning (WIL). WIL is a pedagogical approach that has been used around the world to combine academic understanding, knowledge, and practices into real workplace environments (Patrick et al. 2008). WIL is often used as an umbrella term that encompasses programs, such as cooperative education (co-op), internships, and practicums (Patrick et al. 2008; Gardner and Bartkus 2014). A key feature of WIL is that students are given the opportunity to apply what they have learned in their classrooms to workplaces (Gardner and Bartkus 2014), which in comparison to academic environments are often messy and imperfect (Fullan and Scott 2014).

Under this approach, students are encouraged to identify and utilize workplace codes and conventions (Bowen 2018), engage in reflection about their behaviors (Smith 2012), and learn to problem-solve in real-time (Coll et al. 2009). These work placements are also designed to give students the opportunity to develop a sense of professionalism and ethical accountability (Bowen 2018; McNamara 2013), build adaptability, resilience, and independence (Bowen and Drysdale 2017; Mate and Ryan 2015), and test their character and disposition to see how it impacts their ability to effectively perform their work alongside colleagues who share a common goal (Bowen and Drysdale 2017). As a result of these opportunities, it is believed that individuals who complete WIL programs are more employable after graduation, as they have developed the abilities needed to successfully transition and become engaged in a workplace setting (Billet 2009).

Unfortunately, not only do many educational programs fail to provide students with the skills necessary to make connections between diverse academic programs, so, too, have some WIL programs such as cooperative education been criticized for failing to train students to make the important connections between their educational programs and their work settings (Coll and Zegwaard 2011). Some co-op programs have introduced work reports or special online courses to help students make these connections and thus to function as boundary spanners. For example, the University of Waterloo requires all co-op students to complete a set of courses, called WatPD (Waterloo Professional Development 2019b), designed to aid the integration of student's academic program with what is learned at work. A similar program, EDGE, is available to non-co-op students (Waterloo Professional Development 2019a). EDGE an experiential education program comprised of several courses designed around topics that are relevant to boundary spanning, such as communication, teamwork, conflict resolution, and intercultural skills. Attesting to the benefits of programs such as EDGE, research has shown that students who participate in the program receive higher ratings from employers on their work performance than those who do not (Pretti, Noël, and Waller 2014).

Education, however, is not the only route to becoming a boundary spanner. It is also necessary that individuals have the opportunity to practice and refine these behaviors. On the job, this requires employers to encourage connections both across the organization and outside it. Hsu and colleagues (2007) explain organizations should provide time, resources, and incentives to encourage employees to make connections beyond their own department. At earlier stages in the development of prospective workers, employees should not just be required to work in teams but to be taught the necessary skills for group work and be supervised and mentored as these skills are put into practice.

The Future of Boundary Spanning

Is it important that all students or employees strive to become boundary spanners? Certainly, any kind of team project, whether in school or work, requires some level of boundary spanning, but even there, not all team members need to possess high levels of these abilities. Estry's analysis in Chapter One of Gardner's experience in Thailand is one example that highlights the potential one boundary spanner can have on bringing together a disparate team to achieve success. Certainly, leaders of teams with members who have different backgrounds, education, and experience, and working on complex projects should possess boundary spanning skills.

While it may be premature to draw conclusions from the limited amount of research that has been done on boundary spanning abilities to date, it is clear that strong communication skills are an absolute necessity in the workplace. Moreover, in order to gain respect both within one's own work group as well as groups externally, there is some evidence to suggest that boundary spanners need to be highly competent in their disciplinary jobs. They are likely to be innovative and have high status in their work group or organization. Some personality characteristics have been suggested here, notably openness to experience and conscientiousness. Their educational programs should have provided them with training and opportunities to practice working in groups with diverse backgrounds and different skills. Most important, however, is that they work in an organization with flexible structures that is supportive of employees making connections across boundaries, both internal and external. Such an organization is likely to benefit from the knowledge acquired by their boundary spanners, while the organization that limits boundary crossing of its employees will suffer from reduced innovation and new ideas.

References

Beechler, S., Søndergaard, M., Miller, E., & Bird, A. (2004). Boundary spanning. In H. Lane, M. Maznevski, M. Mendenhall, & J. McNett (Eds.), *The handbook of global management: A guide to managing complexity* (pp. 121–133). Malden: Blackwell Publishing.

Billett, S. (2009). Realising the educational worth of integrating work experiences in higher education. *Studies in Higher Education, 34*(7), 827–843.

Bowen, T. (2018). Becoming professional: Examining how WIL students learn to construct and perform their professional identities. *Studies in Higher Education, 43*(7), 1148–1159.

Bowen, T., & Drysdale, M. T. B. (2017). Introduction. In T. Bowen & M. T. B. Drysdale (Eds.), *Work-Integrated Learning in the 21st Century* (pp. xvii–xxv). Bingley: Emerald Publishing.

Coll, R. K., Eames, C., Paku, L., Lay, M., Hodges, D., Bhat, R., … Martin, A. (2009). An exploration of the pedagogies employed to integrate knowledge in work-integrated learning. *Journal of Cooperative Education & Internships, 43*(1), 14–35.

Coll, R. K., & Zegwaard, K. E. (2011). The integration of knowledge in cooperative and work-integrated education programs. In R. K. Coll & K. E. Zegwaard (Eds.), *International handbook for cooperative and work-integrated education: International perspectives of theory, research and practice* (2nd ed., pp. 297–304). Lowell, MA: World Association for Cooperative Education.

Digman, J. (1990). Personality structure: Emergence of the five-factor model. *Annual Review of Psychology, 41*, 417–440.

Fullan, M., & Scott, G. (2014). *Education PLUS*. Seattle, Washington: Collaborative Impact SPC. Retrieved from www.michaelfullan.ca/wp-content/uploads/2014/09/Education-Plus-A-Whitepaper-July-2014-1.pdf

Gardner, P., & Estry, D. (2017). *A primer on the T-professional*. Michigan: Collegiate Employment Research Institute, Michigan State University.

Gardner, P., & Bartkus, K. R. (2014). What's in a name? A reference guide to work-education experiences. *Asia-Pacific Journal of Cooperative Education, 15*(1), 37–54.

Hsu, S. H., Wang, Y. C., & Tzeng, S. F. (2007). The source of innovation: Boundary spanner. *Total Quality Management and Business Excellence, 18*(10), 1133–1145.

Jernigan, E. (n.d.). *A Renaissance Education for the 21st Century*. Retrieved from https://uwaterloo.ca/knowledge-integration/sites/ca.knowledge-integration/files/uploads/files/KIasRenaissanceEducation.pdf

Judge, T. A., & Bono, J. E. (2000). Five-factor model of personality and transformational leadership. *Journal of Applied Psychology, 85*(5), 751–765.

Leutner, F, Ahmetoglu, G., Akhtar, R., & Chamorro-Premuzic, T. (2014). The relationship between the entrepreneurial personality and the big five personality traits. *Personality and Individual Differences, 63*, 58–63.

Mate, S., & Ryan, M. (2015). Learning through work: How can a narrative approach to evaluation build students' capacity for resilience? *Asia-Pacific Journal of Cooperative Education, 16*(3), 153–161.

McNamara, J. (2013). The challenge of assessing professional competence in work integrated learning. *Assessment & Evaluation in Higher Education, 38*(2), 183–197.

Miller, P. M. (2008). Examining the work of boundary spanning leaders in community contexts. *International Journal of Leadership in Education, 11*(4), 353–377.

Nyhus, E. K., & Pons, E. (2005). The effects of personality on earnings. *Journal of Economic Psychology, 26*(3), 363–384.

Onishi, M. (2016). Measuring nurse managers' boundary spanning: Development and psychometric evaluation. *Journal of Nursing Management, 24*(4), 560–568.

Patrick, C. J., Peach, D., Pockness, C., Webb, F., Fletcher, M., & Pretto, G. (2008). *The WIL (Work integrated learning) report: A national scoping study [Final report]*. Brisbane: Queensland University of Technology.

Pretti, T. J., Noël, T., & Waller, T. G. (2014). *Evaluation of the effectiveness of an online program to help co-op students enhance their employability skills: A study of the University of Waterloo's professional development program (WatPD)*. Toronto: Higher Education Quality Council of Ontario.

Sandmann, L., Jordan, J., Mull, C., & Valentine, T. (2014). Measuring boundary-spanning behaviors in community engagement. *Journal of Higher Education, Outreach and Engagement, 18*(3), 83–104.

Smith, C. (2012). Evaluating the quality of work-integrated learning curricula: A comprehensive framework. *Higher Education Research & Development, 31*(2), 247–262.

Sparrowe, R., Liden, R., Wayne, S., & Kraimer, M. (2001). Social networks and the performance of individuals and groups. *Academy of Management Journal, 44*(2), 316–325.

Steel, G. D., Rinnie, T., & Fairweather, J. (2012). Personality, nations, and innovation: Relationships between personality traits and national innovation scores. *Cross-Cultural Research, 46*(1), 3–30.

Strober, M. H. (2011). *Interdisciplinary conversations: Challenging habits of thought*. Stanford: Stanford University Press.

Tushman, M., & Scanlan, T. (1981). Characteristics and external orientations of boundary spanning individuals. *Academy of Management Journal, 24*(1), 83–98.

Waterloo Professional Development Program. (2019a). *EDGE Students*. Retrieved from https://uwaterloo.ca/professional-development-program/edge-students

Waterloo Professional Development Program. (2019b). *Welcome to WatPD.* Retrieved from https://uwaterloo.ca/professional-development-program/

Williams, P. (2002). The competent boundary spanner. *Public Administration, 80*(1), 103–124.

Wilson, D. (2009). *The future of learning in organizations.* Learning Innovations Laboratories. Cambridge, MA: Harvard Graduate School of Education.

Contributed Author

Dr. Patricia M. Rowe is Professor Emirita of Psychology at the University of Waterloo in Canada. Her research interests in the personnel selection interview, the early work experiences of young graduates, and the effects of work experience on future behavior inevitably attracted her to research on students in the large cooperative education program at Waterloo. In addition, she served as founder and director of the industrial/organizational psychology graduate program, founding member of the Waterloo Centre for the Advancement of Co-operative Education, and dean of Graduate Studies at Waterloo.

Dr. Maureen T. B. Drysdale is Professor of Psychology at St. Jerome's University in the University of Waterloo and Adjunct Professor in Applied Health Studies, School of Public Health and Health Systems at the University of Waterloo. She is also the Director of the Well-Link Research Lab, where she leads a large team of undergraduate interns, graduate research assistants, and collaborators from institutions around the globe who are dedicated to enhancing the mental health and well-being of students during school-to-school and school-to-work transitions. She is also a founding member of the Waterloo Centre for the Advancement of Co-operative Education.

CHAPTER 4

The ME

Marc Hunsaker and Jennifer Rivera

T-students are well-prepared to respond and adapt to an ever-changing career landscape through the acquisition of deep disciplinary/systemic knowledge coupled with the development of boundary-spanning skills. As T-students' broad skills and deep knowledge merge together, they are equipped to more effectively operate across a wide range of disciplines, systems, and professional fields. At the intersection of the T's vertical and horizontal axes is the ME, or knowledge of the self. This chapter will demonstrate how the ME is the critical component of the T because it (a) conceptually holds the other components of the T together, (b) practically describes how T-students are well-positioned to successfully navigate the constantly evolving relationship between college and career, and (c) theoretically aligns with the related literature on academic success and career development.

What Is the ME?

The ME is composed of three overlapping domains of personal development: purpose, awareness, and confidence (PAC). These three developmental domains constitute the basic building blocks that enable T-professionals to articulate their life goals (purpose) and learn with and from others (awareness) to effectively pursue their goals despite struggles and setbacks (confidence). This chapter includes a description of each of these PAC domains, as depicted in Figure 4.1.

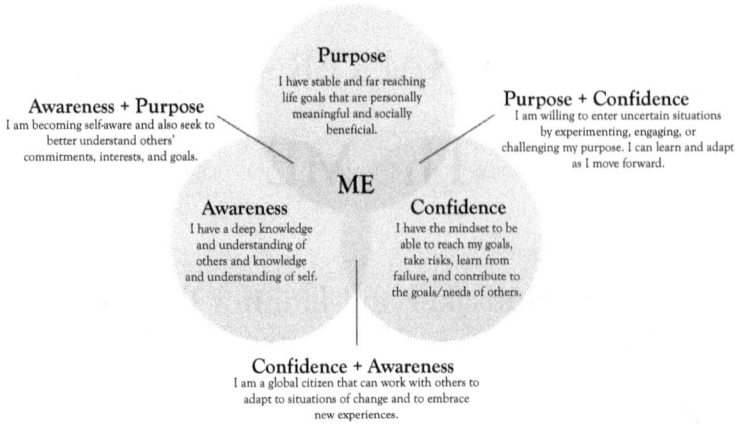

Purpose
I have stable and far reaching life goals that are personally meaningful and socially beneficial.

Awareness + Purpose
I am becoming self-aware and also seek to better understand others' commitments, interests, and goals.

Purpose + Confidence
I am willing to enter uncertain situations by experimenting, engaging, or challenging my purpose. I can learn and adapt as I move forward.

ME

Awareness
I have a deep knowledge and understanding of others and knowledge and understanding of self.

Confidence
I have the mindset to be able to reach my goals, take risks, learn from failure, and contribute to the goals/needs of others.

Confidence + Awareness
I am a global citizen that can work with others to adapt to situations of change and to embrace new experiences.

Figure 4.1 The domains of the ME

Purpose

Within the T, the core developmental domain is *purpose,* which describes the ability to articulate meaningful goals for one's life and career. Purposeful goals are described as being stable, far-reaching, personally meaningful, and socially beneficial (Bronk 2014; Damon 2008). The pursuit of purposeful goals enable T-individuals to experience higher levels of meaning, direction, motivation, and success in their education, career, and life.

Purpose has been shown to have an extremely positive impact upon young people's lives both in and after college. For example, college students who have high levels of purpose typically exhibit higher rates of academic persistence and retention (Yeager et al. 2014), increased engaged and meaningful learning (Malin, Liauw, and Damon 2017; Yeager and Bundick 2009), higher grades and test scores (Duckworth, Peterson, Matthews, and Kelly 2007; Yeager et al. 2014), and have more clarity and confidence about their choice of a major and career (Clydesdale 2015; Dik, Duffy, and Eldridge 2009). Beyond the classroom, the impact of purpose on students' health and wellness is equally impressive. Purpose has been identified as a core component of identity development (Burrow, O'Dell, and Hill 2010), mental health (Steger and Frazier 2005), life satisfaction and hope (Clydesdale 2015), and psychological well-being (Sumner, Burrow, and Hill 2015; Seligman 2011).

Furthermore, young adults who have a strong sense of purpose have been shown to be better prepared for and more successful in life after college, often exhibiting higher levels of satisfaction and well-being into adulthood (Mariano and Vaillant 2012). In fact, having a strong sense of purpose has been shown to be the number one long-term indicator of well-being in life (Sumner et al. 2015). Purpose also has a profound positive impact on a person's relationship with their work. Having purpose is strongly associated with viewing one's work as a *calling* (Dik and Duffy 2012; Dik et al. 2009), which often leads workers to be more motivated, engaged, and satisfied with their work (Wrzesniewski, McCauley, Paul, and Schwartz 1997). Additionally, purposeful adults have been shown to have higher levels of income post-college and higher net-worth over the course of their lives (Hill, Turiano, Mroczek, and Burrow 2016).

The emerging research on purpose is clear: people who have developed a strong sense of purpose are more likely to be happier, healthier, wealthier, more satisfied, and successful in their lives, school, and work. Given the massive positive impact that purpose has on the lives of people in general, and young adults in particular, it is critical for colleges and universities to intentionally promote the purpose development of T-students.

Within the T, purpose is conceptualized by drawing upon the most commonly accepted and utilized definition within the literature: "Purpose is a stable and generalized intention to accomplish something that is at the same time meaningful to the self and consequential for the world beyond the self" (Damon 2008, p. 33). This definition is grounded primarily in the research of developmental psychologists Damon (2008) and Bronk (2014), who identify four critical components of purpose that form a theoretical framework for the T-model. The four components of this purpose framework are enduring commitments, goal-directedness, personal meaningfulness, and prosocial motivations. A description of each of these components and their connection to the development of T-students follow.

Enduring Commitments

The core component of purpose and identity development is a person's enduring commitments. These commitments include a person's core values, worldview beliefs, and primary social responsibilities (Erikson 1980).

To establish a coherent identity, a person must commit to particular beliefs, values, and orientations (Erikson 1980) and these commitments also help to define the individual's purpose through consistent patterns of thinking, behaving, and decision making (Bronk 2014). In this way, enduring commitments function as the roots from which one's sense of purpose emerges. Therefore, it is essential for T-students to begin to intentionally identify some of their core values, beliefs, and social responsibilities as early as possible in their undergraduate journey so that they can also begin to articulate and pursue related goals.

Goal-directedness

Purposeful people are often identified by "having goals and directedness" (Ryff and Singer 2008), persisting toward their goals (Benard 1991), and relating their current activities and experiences to their future goals (Baumeister 1991). The focus on developing, articulating, and pursuing goals is part of what distinguishes purpose from related constructs such as "meaning" or "passion" (Bronk 2014). Additionally, purposeful goals are often characterized as being both stable and far-reaching (Damon 2008). Stable goals should not be understood as a set of specific fixed ambitions (e.g., getting into a top-ranked medical school), but rather as a set of fairly consistent interests within a person's life (e.g., helping people live healthier lives). Far-reaching goals are often described as large-scale aims that are unlikely to be easily achieved within a person's lifetime (e.g., curing cancer, eliminating poverty, elevating political discourse). However, the articulation and pursuit of far-reaching goals encourages T-students to develop a clearer direction for their academic/career interests and increases their motivation to make progress toward these goals.

Personal Meaningfulness

Within the T-model, personal meaningfulness flows from a perceived coherency between a person's commitments and their life goals, particularly their professional aspirations (Dik, Byrne, and Steger 2013). This perspective is based on research that shows that people often draw upon their core values and commitments to justify their actions and identify goals they experience as personally meaningful (Baumeister 1991). In this way, purposeful goals reflect a person's "ultimate concern" (Damon 2008), which provides a clear "...answer to the question *why?* Why are you doing this? Why does it matter to you? Why is it important for me and for the world beyond me?" (p. 33). When people view their work as being aligned with their core commitments, they often identify *noble purposes* within their basic day-to-day responsibilities or tasks that others tend to describe as unenjoyable or tedious parts of their jobs (Bronk 2012). As T-students are able to articulate how their goals are connected to their ultimate concerns, they will develop intrinsic motivations needed to make continual progress toward their far-reaching goals, despite encountering inevitable setbacks and struggles.

Prosocial Motivations

Current research also shows that purpose includes prosocial motivations, often referred to as *beyond-the-self concerns* (Damon 2008). Some researchers have identified beyond-the-self motivations as the most impactful component of purpose into adulthood and the primary factor for a happy and successful life (Dik et al. 2013). Research has shown that beyond-the-self concerns are the component most often underemphasized among young adults (Hill, Burrow, O'Dell, and Thornton 2010), it also shows that young people are able to develop prosocial motivations when given opportunities to engage in educational activities that promote empathy and awareness of others (Yeager et al. 2014). The findings about the importance (and lack) of prosocial motivations among young adults highlight a strategic opportunity for colleges and universities. As college students are encouraged to consider how their life goals could address societal needs, undergraduate education enables graduates to experience happier, more meaningful lives, while also creating socially conscious young adults who are more prepared to be engaged global citizens.

The four-part purpose framework outlined above provides an integrative lens through which to view and promote the purpose development of T-students. This conception of purpose provides a critical link between a students' broad skills (horizontal of the T) and their deep disciplinary and systems knowledge (vertical of the T) by fostering a clearer understanding of *who* they are, *what* they want to do with their lives, and *how* their goals will benefit others. In this way, purpose fosters greater direction, motivation, and meaning to T-students as they envision, articulate, and pursue their academic goals and future career plans. Furthermore, by promoting stable and far-reaching goals, purpose enables T-students to imagine a wider range of potential career pathways and opportunities, which better prepares them to effectively navigate the boundaryless careers and technological disruptions that have become commonplace in the ever-shifting 21st century workforce landscape.

Awareness

Awareness is defined as knowledge and understanding of both self and others. A greater sense of awareness strengthens students' meaning-making of knowledge, skills, and attitudes when working deep and across many disciplines and systems. In a broader sense, awareness is a key factor of emotional intelligence. An increased sense of awareness in one's self and others strengthens self-understanding and increases the ability to proactively monitor one's thoughts, emotions, and behaviors. Awareness enables learners to develop a stronger capacity required to successfully ... navigate systemic changes with a purposeful mindset.

A phrase used in centuries-old mindfulness meditation practices associates self-awareness with *being awake*. When one is *awake* to life, they are in the present moment and more aware of thoughts before they become emotional reactions. Cultivating awareness through mindfulness practices dates back thousands of years; however, it is a practice adopted recently in the U.S. K-12 school systems as a tool to increase emotional stability in youth (Meiklejohn et al. 2012). Because of the increase and success of mindfulness education at the secondary level, upcoming cohorts of college-aged students may have a stronger foundational sense of self-awareness. This foundational awareness can be further developed in higher education through the coupling or integrating of mindfulness practices with traditional instruction For example, purposely enabling students to build self-determination and self-monitoring skills by engaging with the content in different ways, through different types of interactions, or through different advising experiences.

Confidence

Confidence refers to a personal belief in one's ability to effectively pursue their goals. This developmental domain is composed of two primary components: self-confidence and self-efficacy, which align with each of axes of the T-model. Self-confidence and self-efficacy are often used interchangeably, as both are psychological traits that focus on a person's knowledge about how much they know (Fischhoff, Slovic, and Lichtenstein 1977). However, a more nuanced understanding of each term provides a deeper appreciation of and connection between the ME and the T-model. For example, self-confidence is often used as a broad term within the literature, defined as a "measure of one's belief in one's own abilities" (Stankov and Lee 2008), and has been shown to be a primary predictor of students' academic achievement (Stankov, Morony, and Lee 2013). This broad definition of confidence aligns well with broad boundary-spanning skills located within the horizontal axis of the T-model. Self-efficacy is often distinguished from self-confidence in how it focuses on domain-specific abilities (Bandura 1997), including the ability to learn or perform specific skills that are required to be successful in a particular academic or professional field (Komarraju, Swanson, and Nadler 2014; Pajares and Schunk 2001). In this sense, the emphasis of self-efficacy aligns well with the specific deep disciplinary and systems knowledge embedded with the vertical axis of the T-model. Therefore, it is extremely important for T-students to continually develop greater confidence in their specific academic and professional abilities.

Other studies have shown that academic and professional confidence can be situationally induced. Bandura (1997) offers four primary sources that affect the development of self-efficacy: (1) *mastery experiences* offer experiential learning opportunities, which can help T-students build confidence in their knowledge and abilities; (2) *social modeling* offers opportunities for students to learn vicariously through the experiences of their role models; (3) *social persuasion* offers students important guidance and verbal forms of encouragement from others, and (4) *physiological stress* offers students an opportunity to learn how to appropriately manage/reduce stress and interpret physical and emotional reactions to stress as being normal as opposed to indicating a lack of ability.

In the T-model, developing confidence begins with students becoming more certain of their own identity, knowledge, and skills. This growing sense of confidence leads T-students to set challenging goals and remain committed to achieving them despite setbacks and adversity. In these ways, developing deeper confidence will enable T-students to become more comfortable taking risks, embrace a willingness to experiment, and effectively recover from setbacks and learn from failures.

Sensemaking in the ME: Surface Reflection to Deep Reflection

Reflection is a fundamental practice that helps students develop a sense of self and adopt increasingly complex meaning-making structures. Critical or deep reflection assists students to, "… articulate questions, confront bias, examine causality, contrast theory with practice and identify systemic issues all of which helps foster critical evaluation and knowledge transfer" (Ash and Clayton 2009, p. 27). Deep reflection is a practice vital to students' self-regulation (Kegan 1995), which is required to make consistent progress within the three developmental domains of the ME and apply sensemaking to the respective axes of the T-model.

As mentioned earlier, reflective practice in teaching and learning environments dates back over 100 years. Dewey (1910) defined the reflective process in two parts: "(a) a state of perplexity, hesitation, doubt; and (b) an act of search or investigation directed toward bringing to light further facts which serve to corroborate or to nullify the suggested belief." Dewey's notion of reflection was a major concept embedded in constructivist theories of transformative learning popularized in the latter half of the 20th century. More recently Marzano (2007) promoted reflection as a pedagogical macro-strategy that teachers could integrate into learning experiences. Currently, this strategy is a common form of instructional practice utilized in higher education.

An upward trend finds higher educational institutions integrating reflective practice as an instructional tool to assist student understanding. When reflection remains at a superficial level, students' knowledge level rarely exceeds describing course learning experiences. Done correctly, deep or critical reflection strengthens student learning and understanding and is a process where students can connect their experiences to changes in one's self, others, community, and society.

Developmentally appropriate curricular and cocurricular learning experiences, when coupled with critical reflective practices, assist students in cultivating both a clearer sense of self and a clearer sense of their purpose. This internal validation of self is commonly framed through the lens of "self-authorship," which Baxter-Magolda (2001) defines as "the internal capacity to define one's beliefs, identity, and social relations" (p. 269). Providing critical reflection opportunities (via reflective prompts) for students to develop a self-authoring mind helps them to become more confident and aware of their emerging sense of purpose and how their purpose stems from their internal/personal goals, worldviews, values, and beliefs.

Deep Reflection as a Practice

Dewey (1910) described the process of reflection as a messy investigation that is filled with doubt. To diffuse some of this perplexity, multiple opportunities for deep reflection throughout a students' college journey can assist in the development of their purpose, awareness, and confidence. In the T-model, these three developmental domains intentionally overlap, highlighting the inherently synergistic relationships between these capacities and additional deep reflective experiences, which contribute to students' development of the ME.

Purpose + Awareness

The practice of deep reflection enables students to blend awareness with purpose, helping them to more clearly understand how their core commitments could inform and support their academic and professional goals. In becoming more aware about how their core commitments are coherent with their goals, T-learners are becoming more attuned to and motivated by how their immediate educational tasks are connected to their "ultimate concerns" (Damon 2008). In these ways, T-students are developing deeper knowledge about *why* they are doing what they are doing: *why* they are in college, *why* they chose their specific major, and *why* their current educational tasks are important to reach their long-term goals.

Deep reflection also helps T-students to be more aware of how their purposeful goals could fit in the world. Through reflection, students can also continually improve their awareness of the different perspectives, learning styles, and worldviews held by others, and apply this understanding in order to reprocess their own tacit knowledge (Schön 1983). Bringing awareness together with purpose does not mean getting lost in one's self, but rather helps to create a space where one can be more purposeful in considering both personal and group values within their daily decision-making. Students who develop greater awareness from working within a diverse collective system are better prepared to intentionally adapt and stay purposeful in the face of constant sociocultural change (Brown 2007).

Reflective prompts: How do your core commitments inform the academic, professional, and life goals you are currently pursuing? How do your personal commitments, interests, and goals converge or diverge from those of the people you work/live with? How could your abilities and interests address some of the societal needs around you? How can you join in with the work that other people are already doing to address these issues?

Desired learning outcomes of purpose + awareness: T-students will be able to more deeply understand differences, identify opportunities for coherence with others, effectively mobilize resources, and work with others as a team.

Purpose + Confidence

Deep reflection also enables students to become more confident about their emerging sense of purpose and how it fits in the world. The intersection of purpose and confidence is a space where T-students can develop greater confidence in their ability to pursue their goals. Reflection offers learners the opportunity to build confidence by creating practical plans to pursue their purpose, such as setting short-term goals to make progress on their far-reaching goals. The merger of confidence and purpose can also enable students to develop greater perseverance for pursuing their goals in spite of ambiguity and setbacks.

Deep reflection also helps T-students become more confident about the potential synergies that exist between their goals and the goals of others. As students become more confident about the overlap between their skills, values, knowledge, and goals, and those of others, they become more committed to pursuing mutually beneficial relationships with others. In this way, purpose and confidence promotes synergistic relationships between T-students and the people around them, enabling both to achieve more than the sum of their individual parts.

Reflective prompts: Who can help as you pursue your own goals? What can you learn from the people around you? How can others help you learn to take risks, consider creative solutions to problems, and more effectively manage stress as you pursue your goals? Alternatively, who else could potentially benefit from some of your skills, knowledge, and goals? How could you help others to more effectively pursue their goals?

Desired learning outcomes of purpose + confidence: T-students will be able to make concrete plans to pursue their goals, take actions in spite of ambiguity, take risks in spite of failure, and learn from their struggles and mistakes (i.e., "fail forward").

Awareness + Confidence

Intentionally navigating one's purpose in an ever-changing environment requires a blend of awareness and confidence. Systemic change works in collective ways, disrupting the egotistical narrative of *my purpose*. Learning with and from others requires awareness of our own contributions and vulnerabilities as well as a sense of self-reliance to trust in interdependence. Reflective practices in this space socialize learners toward developing an interdependent mind-set that allows them to better embrace complexities of the T-experience.

Reflective prompts: How are different groups, communities, and countries connected and what is your role in this interconnectedness? What values, attitudes, and skills do you possess that allow you to manage and engage with diverse groups and perspectives? What does it mean to be a member of the global community and how do you and others respond to common problems and issues in everyday life?

Desired learning outcomes of awareness + confidence: T-students will have the ability to work with others to effectively address common challenges. Students will grow more confident in standing up for their beliefs, and become more skilled in evaluating the ethics and impacts of their decisions. Students will also be able to adapt to situations of change and embrace new ideas and experiences.

Conclusion

As demonstrated in this chapter, the ME is the most critical component of the T-model because it provides students with the essential goals, motivations, and mindsets, which personally and practically connect the upper and lower axes of the T. Through experiential learning and deep reflection, T-students can develop greater purpose, awareness, and confidence about how their life goals, broad skills, and deep knowledge can transfer to a wide range of contexts and be leveraged to address a wide variety of social/workforce needs.

Working Definitions for the Major Components of the T-model

In the context of the T-model, *deep disciplinary knowledge* is the domain of knowledge, inclusive of foundational knowledge, held by all professionals in that discipline as well as that knowledge unique to a given specialization (subdiscipline) within that domain and encompasses the psychomotor and affective abilities critical to a practitioner's success.

In the context of the T-model, *deep systems knowledge* and its accompanying skill set of *systems thinking* is the understanding of intra- and inter-system complexity that embraces the physical, biological, economic, financial, social, organizational, and political processes, services, units, and events. These comprised resources and interconnected flows and variables, which produce feedback loops and involve human connections. These systems generate their own behavior patterns requiring open, innovative, and flexible thinking and self-learning that embraces other people's perspectives and persistence in the face of external and internal challenges that can impede finding solutions.

Interdisciplinary understanding within the T-model embraces the synthesizing (integrating) the knowledge and modes of thinking from two or more disciplines into one approach to provide novel solutions to multidimensional, complex problems and offer explanations of the world around us whose solutions require new interpretations through learning opportunities centered around originality, personal meaning, creativity and risk-taking (adapted from http://webshare.northseattle.edu/IS/readings/what_is_interdisciplinary_learni.htm).

A *boundary-spanning* individual within the T-model possesses the "ability to develop partnerships and collaboration by building sustainable relationships, managing through influence and negotiation, and seeking to understand motives, roles, and responsibilities" (Williams 2002).

The *ME* component is defined through these three elements:

- *Purpose* is "a stable and generalized intention to accomplish something that is at the same time meaningful to the self and consequential for the world beyond the self."
- *Awareness* is knowledge and understanding of others (empathy) and knowledge of self, one's capabilities—strengths, weaknesses, ways of knowing and understanding—and recognition of the importance of others and the value that diversity brings to the resolution of challenges/problems.
- *Confidence* includes taking risks, *seeing mistakes as necessary trials toward success*, being comfortable and confident in one's knowledge, and seeking and embracing others' knowledge, or suspending one's own mental models in order to consider alternatives thereby being *a secure learner (that is) tolerant of ambiguity*.

References

Ash, S., & Clayton, P. (2009). Generating, deepening, and documenting learning: The power of critical reflection in applied learning. *Journal of Applied Learning in Higher Education, 1*(1), 25–48.

Bandura, A. (1997). *Self-efficacy: The exercise of control.* New York, NY: W H Freeman/Times Books/ Henry Holt & Co.

Baumeister, R. F. (1991). *Meanings of life.* New York, NY: Guilford Press.

Baxter-Magolda, M. (2001). *Making their own way: Narratives for transforming higher education to promote self-development.* Sterling, VA: Stylus.

Benard, B. (1991). *Fostering resiliency in kids: Protective factors in the family, school, and community.* San Francisco: Far West Laboratory for Educational Research and Development.

Brown, M. (2007). *Emergent strategy.* Chico, CA: AK Press.

Bronk, K. C. (2012). A grounded theory of the development of noble youth purpose. *Journal of Adolescent Research, 27*(1), 78–109.

Bronk, K. C. (2014). *Purpose in life: A critical component of optimal youth development.* Dordrecht: Springer.

Burrow, A., O'Dell, A., & Hill, P. (2010). Profiles of a developmental asset: Youth purpose as a context for hope and well-being. *Journal of Youth and Adolescence, 39*(11), 1265–1273.

Clydesdale, T. (2015). *The purposeful graduate: Why colleges must talk to students about vocation.* Chicago: University of Chicago Press.

Damon, W. (2008). *The path to purpose: Helping our children find their calling in life.* New York, NY: Free Press.

Dewey, J. (1910). *How we think.* Boston, MA: D.C. Heath & Co.

Dik, B. J., Byrne, Z. S., & Steger, M. F. (2013). *Purpose and meaning in the workplace.* Washington, DC: American Psychological Association.

Dik, B. J., & Duffy, R. D. (2012*). Make your job a calling: How the psychology of vocation can change your life at work.* West Conshohocken, PA: Templeton Press.

Dik, B. J., Duffy, R. D., & Eldridge, B. M. (2009). Calling and vocation in career counseling: Recommendations for promoting meaningful work. *Professional Psychology: Research and Practice, 40*(6), 625–632.

Duckworth, A. L., Peterson, C., Matthews, M. D., & Kelly, D. R. (2007). Grit: Perseverance and passion for long-term goals. *Journal of Personality and Social Psychology, 92*(6), 1087–1101.

Erikson, E. H. (1980). *Identity and the life cycle.* New York, NY: Norton.

Fischhoff, B., Slovic, P., & Lichtenstein, S. (1977). Knowing with certainty: The appropriateness of extreme confidence. *Journal of Experimental Psychology: Human Perception and Performance, 3*(4), 552–564.

Hill, P. L., Burrow, A. L., O'Dell, A. C., & Thornton, M. A. (2010). Classifying adolescents' conceptions of purpose in life, *The Journal of Positive Psychology, 5*(6), 466–473.

Hill, P. L., Turiano, N., Mroczek, D., & Burrow, A. L. (2016). The value of a purposeful life: Sense of purpose predicts greater income and net worth. *Journal of Research in Personality, 65*, 38–42.

Kegan, R. (1995). *In over our heads: The mental demands of modern life.* Cambridge, MA: Harvard University Press.

Komarraju, M., Swanson, J., Nadler, D. (2014). Increased career self-efficacy predicts college students' motivation, and course and major satisfaction. *Journal of Career Assessment, 22*(3), 420–432.

Malin, H., Liauw, I., & Damon, W. (2017). Purpose and character development in early adolescence. *Journal of Youth and Adolescence, 46*(6), 1200–1215.

Mariano, J. M., & Vaillant, G. E. (2012). Youth purpose among the 'greatest generation'. *The Journal of Positive Psychology, 7*(4), 281–293.

Marzano, R. J. (2007). *The art and science of teaching*. Alexandria, VA: Association for Supervision and Curriculum Development.

Meiklejohn, J., Phillips, C., Freedman, M. L., Griffin, M. L., Biegel, G., Roach, A., & Saltzman, A. (2012). Integrating mindfulness training into K-12 education: Fostering the resilience of teachers and students. Mindfulness, 3(4), 291-307. https://doi.org/10.1007/s12671-012-0094-5

Pajares, F., & Schunk, D. (2001). Self-beliefs and school success: Self-efficacy, self-concept, and school achievement. In R. Riding & S. Rayner (Eds.), *Self-perception*. London: Ablex Publishing.

Ryff, C. D., & Singer, B. H. (2008). Know thyself and become what you are: A eudaimonic approach to psychological well-being. *Journal of Happiness Studies, 9*(1), 13–39.

Seligman, M. E. P. (2011). *Flourish: A visionary new understanding of happiness and well being*. New York, NY, US: Free Press.

Stankov, L., & Lee, J. (2008). Confidence and cognitive test performance. *Journal of Educational Psychology, 100*(4), 961–976.

Stankov, L., Morony, S., & Ping Lee, Y. (2013). Confidence: The best non-cognitive predictor of academic achievement? *International Journal of Experimental Educational Psychology, 34*(1).

Schön, D. (1983). *The Reflective Practitioner: How professionals think in action*. New York, NY: Basic Books.

Steger, M., & Frazier, P. (2005). Meaning in life: One link in the chain from religiousness to well-being. *Journal of Counseling Psychology, 52*(4), 574–582.

Sumner, R., Burrow, A. L., & Hill, P. L. (2015). Identity and purpose as predictors of subjective well-being in emerging adulthood. *Emerging Adulthood, 3*(1), 46–54.

Wrzesniewski, A., McCauley, C., Rozin, P., & Schwartz, B. (1997). Jobs, careers, and callings: People's relations to their work. *Journal of Research in Personality, 31*(1), 21–33.

Yeager, D. S., & Bundick, M. J. (2009). The role of purposeful work goals in promoting meaning in life and in schoolwork during adolescence. *Journal of Adolescent Research, 24*(4), 423–452.

Yeager, D., Henderson, M., Paunesku, D., Walton, G., D'Mello, S., Spitzer, B., & Duckworth, A. (2014). Boring but important: A self-transcendent purpose for learning fosters academic self-regulation. *Journal of Personality and Social Psychology, 107*(4), 559–580.

Contributed Authors

Marc Hunsaker Ph.D., is the Dean of Personal and Professional Development at Berry College in Rome, Georgia. In this role, Marc works with a wide range of campus partners to create educational experiences aimed at promoting students' purpose development. He is also involved in the development of innovative programs, curricula, and tools that encourage college students to apply a life-design thinking approach to their professional exploration and planning. His research focuses on how young adults come to view their work as a vocational calling and learn to experience more meaning, purpose, and value in their work

Jennifer "Jeno" Rivera is the Director of the Liberty Hyde Bailey Scholars Program (BSP) in the College of Agriculture and Natural Resources at Michigan State University. The BSP is a program that supports a university undergraduate minor in Leadership in Integrated Learning. She is also an Associate Professor of Community Engagement in the Residential College in the Arts and Humanities and a coactive professional coach for faculty and staff at MSU. Her scholarship identifies teaching and learning components that impend or foster learning through experience. She collaborates in the development, implementation, and evaluation of innovative, high-impact educational programs that promote self-directed learning.

PART II

CHAPTER 5

Hope Is Not a Strategy: On the Need to Design for T-outcomes

Jeffrey T. Grabill

The emergence of massively online open courses (MOOCs)—or at least the most recent, highly commercialized, and venture-funded versions of the MOOC—created yet another moment to question education, specifically how education happens and how humans adapt to these educational advances. Most reacted dismissively to the claims that MOOCs would be disruptive to higher education, yet their influence continues. MOOCs emphasized the underlying, almost tacit understanding that education is a function of information transfer—the delivery of "content" from an expert (teacher) to a novice (student).

Whether or not faculty find the notion that education is simply information transfer, an understanding of what education *is* and *does* is often shared. A fair number of university faculty understand their teaching as content delivery and the primary goal of education is the assimilation of content. Here is where the early commercial MOOC evangelists and the persistent education technology disruptors are correct: if education is a process of content delivery, then any collection of available technologies can perform better, faster, and more inexpensively than any individual instructor or collective university. Coursera, a powerhouse deliverer of MOOCs, provides educational opportunities to over 30 million people around the world in collaboration with over 200 traditional universities, including Michigan State University.

Yet there is another powerful and persistent view that translates education and learning in terms of relationships. The T-model aligns with this view of education because it is grounded in relationships—between ideas and systems—and that it is resolutely student-focused. This chapter dwells on the notion of how purpose plays out in student learning. The fundamental argument; however, is that the only way to get to high-quality learning experiences likely to produce a key outcome such as *purpose* is via careful, participatory design. As an example, Michigan State University created an opportunity to design learning experiences that seem particularly well attuned to engaging students and faculty in questions of purpose: a worthwhile outcome that requires a deep commitment to produce.

Pulling from the T: ME

The collection of chapters in this publication uses the T-professional "as an organizing principle, a vision or framework that embraces efforts to create a strong liberally educated college graduate/professional" (Gardner and Estry 2017, p. 2). The principle that is the focus of this particular chapter is what holds the T together: the ME. Gardner and Estry (2017) argue that the ME is a function of "three interlocking dimensions consisting of purpose, confidence, and awareness" and that it "holds all the other components [of the T] together. The ME is critical to developing the ability to function as a T-professional and is in part the individual's ability to understand core values and motivations" (p. 24). The authors continue their explanation of the ME, which requires a substantial degree of continuing exploration in defining and refining purpose and understanding one's individual and spectator value. Developing the ME demands confidence to take risks and eschew the familiar to discover and expand one's purpose. Michigan State University, like many higher education institutions, spends a great deal of time working with students on *purpose*, which is a significant part of the ME construction. The university introduces dialog on *purpose* at orientation, during academic advising, through the work of career services, and in ways the university engages students in their living units (residence halls). This work is shared by faculty and administrative educators across campus who understand the priority of helping students develop a sense of purpose.

Where the focus on ME is less visible at Michigan State University is in the curriculum. The argument in this chapter is that developing components of the ME constitutes one of the most transformative design principles for undergraduate experiences. To echo Sarasvathy (2003) to help students know *who they are, what they know*, and *who they know* might be the most important learning outcome students can develop. Sarasvathy's (2003) essay on "Entrepreneurship as a Science of the Artificial" is worth reading, as these three categories of knowledge are what he calls *the means* of the entrepreneur. He goes on to characterize entrepreneurs in this way: "They know who they are, what they know and whom they know—their own traits, tastes and abilities, the knowledge corridors they are in, and the social networks they are a part of" (p. 208). These are the characteristics of an *effectuator* (Sarasvathy 2003), the sort of business professional who doesn't worry about predicting the future or about reducing risks before acting because an *effectuator* is involved in the project of making the future.

Developing the mindset of an *effectuator*—one possible way to describe what the ME looks like—is exceptionally valuable. It describes the characteristics of agency an individual should aspire to possess. If universities want students to understand themselves as creators of a shared future, then universities should design for the ME, asking themselves *"What are the learning experiences needed to develop ME?"* The remainder of this chapter will explore this question, looking at a design project that places the ME of the T at the center. Many curriculum reform efforts focus on mainly on the undergraduate core curriculum, but the space in which the development of ME might be most powerful is in a student's major coursework, where analytical thinking, systems thinking, and problem solving are most activated.

Hacking the Major

At present, one of Michigan State University's most compelling curriculum design inquiries is composed of a set of undergraduate, interdisciplinary, experiential courses. One course focuses on new approaches to wildlife conservation in Africa (*Snares to Wares*), a second explores anaerobic digestion as a solution to handling food waste (*The Food Waste Challenge*), and the third focuses scientific communication as students design art proposals for the Rachana Rajendra Neotropical

Migrant Bird Sanctuary (*Wildlife Sanctuary: Communicating Science through Art*). In each experience, students participating are advanced undergraduates going beyond simply completing core requirements. This is rare—at least at a large, public institution. In addition, participating faculty are working across disciplinary silos, some co-teaching for the first time in their careers. While each experience is grounded in one or two disciplinary contexts, the courses are open to students from any major.

All three undergraduate, interdisciplinary, experiential courses are the first iteration of what is intended to be a space for students to engage in deeply experiential and cross-disciplinary learning with faculty and students from multiple areas of campus. The outcomes of experiences such as these are transformative at precisely the ME space in a student's development. In observations to date, researchers assessing the impact of experiential courses have noted considerable change since the classes began in 2018–19, as students and faculty have been engaged in new pedagogical approaches. In *The Food Waste Challenge* and *Wildlife Sanctuary* courses, for instance, student engagement and participation is higher; teams and individuals have taken ownership of their areas of responsibility and move independently of faculty direction; and faculty have shifted from delivering step-by-step content to coaching teams as students become more responsible for their learning experience and more able to manage their own projects (E. Louson and B. Heinrich, field note observation 2019).

Snares to Wares is an experimental course that has run for two semesters, so there are more outcomes to draw from, both from inquiries led by faculty, and most recently, by the students themselves. As the original faculty team describes the experience, "our desire was to organize the students participating in this course into cross-disciplinary teams as a method for facilitating co-learning of content involving:

1. the principles of conservation and sustainability,
2. ethical engagement with local communities in the Global South,
3. marketing, media, and engagement, and
4. business and value chain properties" (Heinrich, Lauren, Montgomery, Mudumba, and Logan 2013, p. 1).

In the spring semester of 2019, a team of student researchers were interested in the impact of the *Snares to Wares* course(s) on the academic and career development of students in both cohorts, examining development through a participant survey and postsurvey reflection. The researchers found that "students underwent a series of professional, educational, and personal development indicating that the degree of student success was heavily influenced by intellectual ownership and interdisciplinary collaboration" (Green et al. 2019, n.p.). More specifically, the researchers found that students were confident in their development in unsurprising areas (e.g., teamwork and communication) given the nature of the work. A much more important set of findings suggest something more powerful: students wanted to continue involvement in the Snares Initiative beyond their course completion (Green et al. 2019, n.p.). The faculty responded by creating a mentor component from course to course, and currently there is a small cohort from the first iteration of the *Snares to Wares* course serving as mentors in this semester's version of the experience. All students surveyed in the current cohort expressed interest in staying involved. Furthermore, 50 percent of the students surveyed have changed their postgraduation plans since enrolling in the *Snares to Wares* course. It is this phenomena, which was visible anecdotally in the first cohort, that is most interesting to those involved in the project (Green et al. 2019, n.p.). Students report high levels of engagement, confidence, and professional growth, and perhaps most interesting is the fact that students report plans to change their trajectory for the future as influenced by course involvement. While the sample size is small, the reflective narratives strongly suggest that perhaps the key outcome of these experiences has been a stronger sense of ME in these students. They have more confidence and possess a greater sense of awareness of the world and their place in it. Franziska Trede (2012) notes the importance of identity development such as this and argues for the development of professional identity within work situations connected to formal education (e.g., internships). These course experiences are quite different in that the *work* takes place within the context of a formal educational moment—a class and classroom. This raises the possibility that identity development either professionally or quasi-professionally is possible outside a work experience.

Gravity, Ownership, Relationship, and Place

Why did the set of undergraduate, interdisciplinary, and experiential courses seem to produce these outcomes? To be sure, the courses (and their related outcomes) represent what have come to be known as "high-impact learning" practices (Kuh and O'Donnell 2013). But it is possible that something more is going on here, and that something more goes right to the heart of ME. The team working on understanding the student impact of participating in the *Snares to Wares* initiative believes that the outcomes are a function of gravity, ownership, relationships, and place, a new construct that they are developing based on their ongoing analysis of the *Snares to Wares* initiative:

- *Gravity*: The notion that the faculty-led project at the core of the course is bigger than the class, which enables students to connect to and develop a passion for the project.
- *Ownership*: The commitment to build trust, spaces and structures for exploration, which enables students to develop a sense of meaning, and frees them to act in ways not common in their education and perhaps unexpected relative to the design of the experience itself. This ownership is created simply by faculty stepping away from the directing process, acting more as facilitators of active learning, coaching rather than directing students through the learning process.
- *Relationships*: The intentional design of an environment conducive to risk and growth, which enables students to try new things, including the development of deep relationships with people and ideas.
- *Place*: The purposeful connection to physical space (both near, where students work together, and far, the place where the project lives in people's lives), which enables students to develop emotional and affective attachments to spaces (and relationships).[1]

---

[1] This particular conceptualization is that of Bill Heinrich, the Head of Assessment in the Hub for Innovation in Learning and Technology. This work currently lives in manuscripts being prepared for publication.

HOPE IS NOT A STRATEGY   63

Clearly these ideas reinforce each other, yet they are present in the assessment as independent factors. These dynamics are visible in the student and faculty reflections. As one of the faculty noted, "Relationships guided social and pedagogical structures including the project based experiential learning and agile teams for collaboration and the trust between students and teachers necessary for the planned structures to operate" (Heinrich et al. 2013, p. 16). Those relationships came fundamentally in two forms: (1) the partnerships required to facilitate the learning and (2) the relationships between ideas, which might be understood as the content of a course. As one student noted, "I found myself engaged in fields I never knew I could contribute to and engaged with people I had never crossed paths with at Michigan State" (Heinrich et al. 2013, p. 16). And of course, it was perhaps the peer learning that had the biggest impact:

> [W]e have learned from one another in a way we would not have been able without this class. Our coaches and every member of this initiative were so invested in making this a memorable experience; we were able to bring musicians from Pakwach, we were able to impact not only MSU but Uganda and much more than that, our own lives. (Heinrich et al. 2013, p. 16)

As another participant noted, "Trust between students and faculty helped create a novel learning experience" (Heinrich et al. 2013, p. 16).

Again, nearly any high-impact learning experience can and often does produce meaningful outcomes. The developing Michigan State University model is in many ways well understood as a high-impact learning practice, and even more importantly, easy to imagine (though difficult to implement) at nearly any university. The work to date suggests that perhaps something important is happening in these experiences that universities should be more intentional in designing for, and that is explicitly developing ME as a primary outcome. As Gardner and Estry (2017) suggest, the T-model does not merely mean adding professional abilities and work-based experiences to the curriculum but taking it many steps further.

Indeed, it is a mistake to believe that faculty and students will somehow find their way to constructing learning experiences that are likely to produce T-students. One of the fundamentals of traditional higher education is that *faculty own the curriculum*, and while that is very much the case at Michigan State University, this doesn't mean that the institution should simply hope that faculty design in a particular direction—or that *design* actually describes the process that results in a learning experience. As a design organization, the Hub is focused on a collaborative, inclusive, and intentional design process. That design work begins with faculty and students (and students are less commonly present than one might expect or hope), but also includes assessment experts, learning designers, and stakeholders such as department chairs and assistant deans. As a model, the T requires the innovative and intentional use of technology, space, and context to design learning experiences that can be integrated to facilitate a learner's development into a T (p. 1). Learning experiences such as this require both design theory and a design practice to produce appropriate outcomes. Simply hoping that a curriculum will help produce the ME, for example, is insufficient and likely to disappoint. The efforts at Michigan State University were certainly intended to be innovative and intentional with regard to technology, space, and context, and the result to date has been a strong and persistent signal that students now have more confidence, possess a greater sense of awareness of the world and their place in it, and therefore, are more purposeful as human beings. An outcome such as this is worth designing for, and the T-model provides the necessary pattern for such designs.

References

Gardner, P., & Estry, D. (2017). *A Primer on the T-professional*. E. Lansing, MI: Michigan State University. Retrieved from http://ceri.msu.edu/wp-content/uploads/2018/03/Primer-on-the-T-professional.pdf

Green, A., Blommel, C., Miller, S., Firn, C., Raupp, J., Ortiz-Calo, W., ... Montgomery, R. (2019, April 5). *The benefit of experiential and interdisciplinary learning programs on students' academic and career development*. Research Poster presented at the Michigan State University Undergraduate Research and Arts Forum. East Lansing, Michigan.

Heinrich, W., Lauren, B., Montgomery, R., Mudumba, T., & Logan, S. (2013). *A Model of a High Impact Practice for Interdisciplinary Teaching and Learning*. Unpublished manuscript, 1.

Kuh, G., & O'Donnell, K. (2013). *Ensuring quality & taking high-impact practices to scale with case studies by sally reed.* Washington, DC: American Association of Colleges & Universities. Retrieved from https://aacu.org/leap

Sarasvathy, S. D. (2003). Entrepreneurship as science of the artificial. *Journal of Economic Psychology, 24,* 203–220.

Trede, F. (2012). Role of work-integrated learning in developing professionalism and professional identity. *Asia-Pacific Journal of Cooperative Education, 13*(3), 159.

Contributed Author

Jeff Grabill serves Michigan State University as the Associate Provost for Teaching, Learning, and Technology, where he remains a Professor of Rhetoric and Professional Writing. Grabill is responsible for facilitating innovation in learning via his role as Director of the Hub for Innovation in Learning and Technology and educator professional development through MSU's Academic Advancement Network.

CHAPTER 6

Academic and Student Affairs Together: Breaking Organizational Silos

Marianna Savoca and Kelley D. Bishop

The structure of traditional universities is unable to produce the T-talent organizations now demand. Advances in artificial intelligence, automation, and the expanded application of agile frameworks to business processes are revolutionizing work, requiring new thinking, new workplace organization, and different ways of operating (Sherman, Edison, Rehberg, and Danoesastro 2017). To ensure that graduates develop the skills and knowledge they need to thrive amidst these advances and within the new multidisciplinary workplace, colleges and universities must create more "crossover learning between departments and disciplines" (Sigelman, Bittle, Markow, and Francis 2019, p. 18). While this idea may seem daunting, transformation of existing structures is within our reach; higher education (HE) is equipped to handle the change. "The strength of higher education in meeting this challenge is that almost all of the skills in demand are already taught in colleges or training institutions. The raw materials are there. The problem is that many of these skills are in curricula or programs that are siloed off from each other" (Sigelman et al. 2019, p. 18). These silos hinder large-scale, timely change from occurring.

Why Do We Have Silos?

The word *silo* comes from a Greek word, συρος, referring to a pit, or something to keep things separate (Oxford English Dictionary n.d.). Silos are commonly associated with the agricultural application, to separate grains; yet there is also an organizational interpretation. According to Tett (2016), organizational "silos are fundamentally a cultural phenomenon," (p. 19) arising from the history, traditions, and ways in which societies have organized themselves.

University silos emerged unintentionally, resulting from professional expertise as faculty specialized in disciplinary knowledge and research (Cohen and Kisker 2010). Concerns about specializations were raised as early as 1937 by student personnel scholars who suggested that colleges give more attention to students' personal, spiritual, health, and vocational development (American Council on Higher Education 1937). The student affairs profession emerged to address these concerns, creating two distinct branches of HE work: faculty focused on research, scholarship, and discipline-based classroom instruction [depth of the T], and student affairs administrators focused on the holistic development of students outside the classroom [breadth of the T].

What Happens When Organizations Become Siloed?

Literature suggests that silos, while appropriate for agriculture, are not viable for other types of business. Silos within companies prevent communication, confuse roles and responsibilities, and limit the sharing of information, expertise, and resources across divisions, frequently obstructing change and hindering innovation (Lemonedes 2018; Tett 2016). When bureaucracies form (Kuh et al. 2006; Reisinger 2016) and organizations falter, the risk of divisional competition increases, deepening the divide and pitting organizational subcommunities against each other (Tett 2016).

University silos create similar challenges of limited contact and communication, and cursory knowledge of the roles each stakeholder group plays in supporting student success. Internal rivalries, superficial collaborations, and an obligatory nod to shared goals emerge (Arcellus 2013). Such divisions result in inefficiency, duplication of services, and limited ability to see large-scale external changes, preventing timely organizational adaptation (Kuh et al. 2006). Most problematic is that siloed institutions force students to navigate a disconnected environment.

Overcoming Silos

Gulati (2007) recommends four strategies to disrupt silos: (1) *coordination*: leveraging shared expertise and joint problem-solving across siloed units; (2) *cooperation*: accountability metrics that value team vs. individual success; (3) *capability*: finding or creating positions requiring boundary spanning understanding; and (4) *connection*: developing external partnerships in support of customer needs.

Disrupting silos through *coordination* takes place when academic and student affairs communicate regularly about shared student concerns, as in the case of cross-divisional committees tackling a range of campuswide challenges. *Cooperation* involves joint accountability for student persistence, where metrics prompt synergistic activities focused on outcomes. *Capability* silo disruption might include provisions in job descriptions for personnel whose roles require boundary spanning activities and intimate knowledge of others' work, and disrupting silos through *connections* could include contributions from staff in advancement, alumni relations, and economic development. Gulati (2010) calls this the outside-in approach, referring to the primary focus on the customer. In HE, our customer, or client, is the student. If student success is truly a shared priority, organizational boundaries will blur as compatible goals and equally held accountability emerge. If HE views the silo concept through the lens of the T, individual disciplines could be categorized as systems silos—distinct vertical hierarchies connected through boundary spanning elements of holistic student engagement bridging the top of T.

Blurring Organizational Lines

A study by Gallup (2014) showed that six key experiences positively impact students' postgraduate workplace engagement: (1) having a professor who made learning exciting, (2) having a professor who took interest in them as a person, (3) having a mentor, (4) working on a semester-long project, (5) having an internship or job where they applied classroom learning, and (6) being extremely active in cocurriculars. These six key experiences involve both academic and nonacademic support, with no clear distinction between inside and outside the classroom. Out-of-classroom experiences such as research, internships, and leadership-focused roles, have all been found empirically to contribute to student learning (Kuh 1995). In *Learning Reconsidered,* Keeling (2004) urged colleges to help students connect the dots between their general education, major coursework, and out-of-class experiences, emphasizing that "learning, development, and identity formation can no longer be considered as separate from each other; they are interactive and shape each other as they evolve" (p. 8). Terenzini, Pascarella, and Blimling (1999) assert that "students' out of class experiences appear to be far more influential in students' academic and intellectual development than many faculty members and student affairs administrators think" (p. 618). These authors suggest that HE embrace a new learning-centered culture where academic and student affairs are equal partners in the writ-large educational mission of colleges and universities: serving the public good (Seligson 2015).

Shared coordination, cooperation, and responsibility for achieving the mission does not mean that deep expertise would or should be eliminated. Applying the T-framework with the student at the center (the ME), the primary faculty role can be seen in the vertical aspect of the T, and the primary student affairs practitioner role in the horizontal aspect. Collaborative, boundary-crossing initiatives that echo T-approaches occur across campus, including first-year seminars and credit-bearing transition courses (O'Connor, Levy, and Polnariev 2016), residential hall tutoring programs (Hossler, Kuh, and Olsen 2001), career development that is infused within the curriculum (Granovskaya et al. 2016), and faculty advisement of student organizations (Komives 2019). Applied learning activities, such as research, internships, service learning, global experiences, and capstone projects are other examples of high-impact practices that involve collaboration across organizational lines (McClellan, Creager, and Savoca 2018) and positively contribute to student success (Kuh 2008). Martin and Rees will discuss work-integrated learning in Chapter 9; therefore, this chapter will highlight living-learning programs as a high-impact practice to develop the T, involving collaboration between academic and student affairs.

Living-Learning Programs

Living-learning programs (LLPs) incorporate topical or academically based themes and build community through common learning. LLPs have been around since the late 1920s but have increased in popularity with more than 600 in existence as of 2009 (Buell, Love, and Yao 2017; Brower and Inkelas 2010; Inkelas, Jessup-Anger, Benjamin, and Wawrzynski 2018). LLPs are instituted for different reasons, but their very name suggests intentional collaboration between academic and student affairs. The thematic focus of LLPs fosters tightly knit social environments and meaningful engagement with faculty. Studies have shown that LLPs are effective at imparting a greater sense of institutional belonging among first-year students, especially during the initial six to ten weeks when many struggle to enculturate into college life. Some institutions have produced measurable improvements in the retention of underrepresented students through LLPs (Inkelas, Daver, Vogt, and Leonard 2007).

Researchers have also noted how LLP learning outcomes resonate with academicians and employers. The National Study of Living-Learning Programs (NSLLP) found students who lived in LLPs applied more critical thinking and took greater advantage of opportunities to apply knowledge to new settings (Brower and Inkelas 2010). The relevance of the NSLLP's findings to the AACU's *Liberal Education and America's Promise* (Humphreys and Davenport 2005) initiative suggests LLPs have potential to accentuate student learning in ways traditionally taught curricula do not.

Many large state institutions offer a variety of academically oriented LLPs. The Honors College LLP at the University of Maryland, for example, enrolls 1,000 first-year students annually and offers two- and four-year programs organized into tracks that include *Advanced Cybersecurity Experience*; *Design Culture and Creativity*; *Entrepreneurship and Innovation*; *Honors Humanities*; and *Integrated Life Sciences* (University of Maryland, n.d.). Team projects require students to collaborate across academically diverse boundaries and draw upon the disciplinary knowledge of each team member. The Honors College expects graduates to be *critically self-reflective, ethically aware, intellectual and creative risk-takers,*

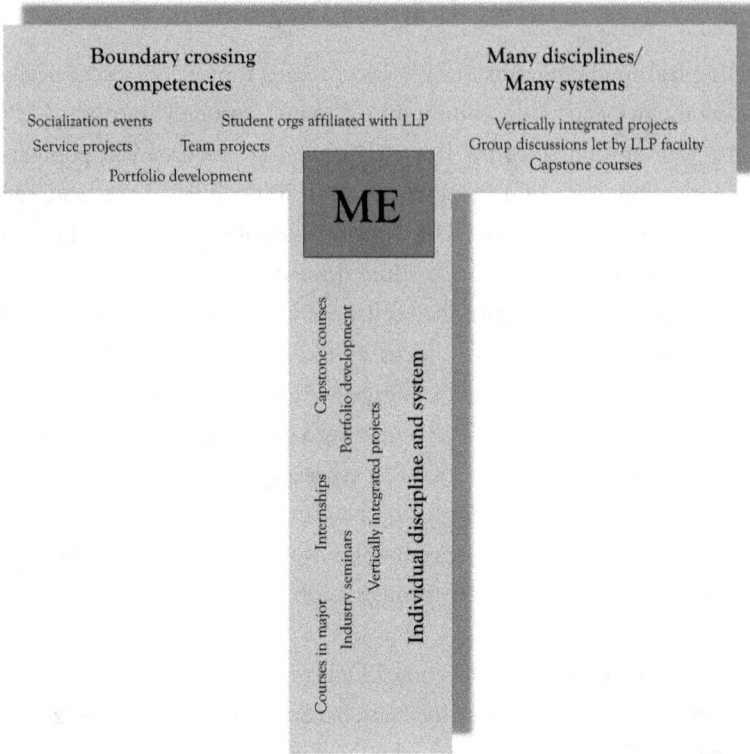

Figure 6.1 T-Professional model

and *collaborative* (University of Maryland, n.d.), reinforcing the T in that solutions to problems require expertise from multiple disciplines.

The cocurricular aspects of LLPs align with the horizontal component of the T-model, specifically designed to foster collaborative skills and a team-minded orientation (see Figure 6.1).

Most programs engage participants in a set of organized activities outside of classes, sometimes planned by the students themselves (Inkelas et al. 2018). Although some activities serve a social purpose, others align with program goals and are intended to impart foundational skills like critical thinking, research, leadership, and social awareness. For example, in the *Women In Natural Sciences* LLP at the University of Texas, participants serve as elementary and secondary school tutors and mentors to female students, inspiring some to pursue STEM-related careers (University of Texas, n.d.). The program enhances participants' ability to effectively convey scientific knowledge to others, increases awareness of challenges in the K–12 environment, and promotes an appreciation of different learning styles, while group reflection exercises reinforce the element of collaboration as essential to progress.

Other activities are geared around projects that build upon ideas or theories in the LLP curriculum. The University of Wisconsin's StartUp Learning Community organizes an annual 100-Hour Challenge contest designed to repurpose surplus materials from labs and classrooms. The event manifests three elements of entrepreneurship: "having an idea, taking action and creating value" (University of Wisconsin, n.d.). For the student organizers, the event develops collaboration, planning, and execution skills while fostering an entrepreneurial spirit. Although students outside LLPs have opportunities to participate in similar cocurricular activities, the experience of LLP students may be fundamentally different because connections between curricular and cocurricular elements are more purposeful.

Another distinguishing feature of some LLPs is the requirement of a summative project at the end of the program in the form of a thesis, a capstone course, or a portfolio. Requiring students to reflect upon pivotal lessons, knowledge, and competencies increases the likelihood that they will connect the dots across their college experience (Inkelas et al. 2018). When these projects involve a presentation to program leaders and peers, students practice articulating what they have learned and why it is meaningful beyond the confines of the LLP program. Peers gain an appreciation of their fellow students, which reinforces another important precept in T-thinking: the ability to recognize the value others bring to the table (Gardner and Estry 2017).

Unfortunately, few LLPs tie their core goals and objectives to career development or workplace preparation. Instead, most focus on academic or social transitions into college, engendering a sense of institutional belonging and cultural diversity (Inkelas et al 2018). However, the structures around which these programs are built stimulate growth within various dimensions of the T-model. While the authors have not yet found explicit references to the T-model within any existing LLPs, their constructs parallel T-concepts. LLPs hold great potential to develop students simultaneously across both axes of the T-model and help the ME component—the focus on the individual—emerge as a unifying interconnecting element.

For the continued success of LLPs, key influencers must espouse a more T-construct, even if they do not invoke the model itself. When authority figures reinforce why cultivating abilities along both the axes matters, those abilities become integrated into the college experience. The extent to which an institution is intentional and transparent about developing the full capacity of students, their mastery of disciplinary knowledge coupled with boundary-crossing competencies may determine the degree to which they achieve their loftiest educational goals.

More Bridges, Fewer Silos

In recapping this chapter, it is apparent that siloed organizations are not optimal, yet universities have a long history of siloed divisions to overcome. Academic and student affairs share the goal of student success (Komives 2019; Kuh et al. 2006) and have noteworthy examples of collaboration, cooperation, capability, and connection supporting dismantling their organizational silos. Partnership is key to this dismantling (Arcelus 2011).

The T-professional may be significant to this effort in two ways. First, it provides a rationale for collaborating across organizational boundaries to create optimal student learning outcomes. Second, it represents a way HE should conduct its work—that faculty and student affairs personnel should themselves exhibit T-behaviors. To better understand each other's work and unique challenges, HE must keep the overarching shared goal of student success front of mind, with clear signals from everyone about the knowledge and skills students will need in the hybrid economy (Sigelman et al. 2019). Also necessary is the need for HE to explicitly signal the ways in which students are developing their T-limbs through in-class and out-of-class learning experiences.

References

American Council on Higher Education. (1937). *1937 Student personnel point of view.* Washington, DC: NASPA

Arcelus, V. J. (2011). Transforming our approach to education: Cultivating partnerships and dialogue. In P. M. Magolda & M. B. B. Magolda (Eds.), *Contested issues in student affairs* (pp. 61–74). Sterling, VA: Stylus.

Brower, A. M., & Inkelas, K. K. (2010). Living learning: One high-impact educational practice we now know a lot about. *Liberal Education, 96*(2), 36–42.

Buell, K. J., Love, V. L., & Yao, C. W. (2017). Living-learning programs through the years: A reflection on partnership between students, faculty, and student affairs. *The Journal of College and University Student Housing, 44*(1), 86–101.

Cohen, A. M., & Kisker, C. B. (2010). Mass higher education in the era of American Hegemony: 1945–1975. In *The shaping of American higher education*. San Francisco, CA: Jossey-Bass.

Gallup Inc. (2014). Great jobs, great lives: The 2014 Gallup-Purdue index report. Washington, D.C.: Gallup and Purdue University.

Gardner, P., & Estry, D. (2017). *A primer on the T-professional*. Lansing, MI: Collegiate Employment Research Institute, Michigan State University.

Granovskaya, Y., Givens, L., Buoy, J., DeFranco, T., DePhilippis, S., Di Renzo, E. M., ... Levy, M. A. (2016). Curricular infusion of career development. In M. A. Levy & B. A. Polnariev (Eds.), *Academic and student affairs collaboration: Creating a culture of student success*. New York, NY: Rutledge.

Gulati, R. (2007). Silo busting. *Harvard Business Review, 85*(5), 98–108.

Gulati, R. (2010). *Reorganize for resilience: Putting customers at the center of your business*. Cambridge, MA: Harvard Business Press.

Hossler, D., Kuh, G. D., & Olsen, D. (2001). Finding fruit on the vines: Using higher educational research and institutional research to guide institutional policies and strategies. Part II. *Research in Higher Education, 42*(2), 223–235.

Humphreys, D., & Davenport, A. (2005). What really matters in college: How students view and value liberal education. *Liberal Education, 91*(3), 36–43.

Inkelas, K. K., Daver, Z. E., Vogt, K. E., & Leonard, J. B. (2007). Living–learning programs and first-generation college students' academic and social transition to college. *Research in Higher Education, 48*(4), 403–434.

Inkelas, K. K., Jessup-Anger, J. E., Benjamin, M., & Wawrzynski, M. R. (2018). *Living learning communities that work: A research-based model for design, delivery, and assessment*. Sterling, VA: Stylus.

Keeling, R. P. (Ed.). (2004). *Learning reconsidered: A campus-wide focus on the student experience*. Washington DC: National Association of Student Personnel Administrators, American College Personnel Association.

Komives, S. R. (2019). Moving beyond the silos. [Special anniversary issue]. *NASPA Leadership Exchange*, 38–40.

Kuh, G. D. (1995). The other curriculum: Out-of-class experiences associated with student learning and development. *Journal of Higher Education, 66*(2), 123-155.

Kuh, G. D. (2008). *High-impact educational practices: What are they, who has access to them, and why they matter*. Washington, D.C.: Association of American Colleges and Universities.

Kuh, G. D., Kinzie, J., Buckley, A. J., Bridges, B. K., & Hayek, J. C. (2006). *What matters to student success: A review of the literature commissioned report for the national symposium on postsecondary student success. Spearheading a dialogue on student success*. Washington, DC: National Postsecondary Cooperative. Retrieved from http://nces.ed.gov/npec/kuh_team_report.pdf

Lemonedes, G. H. (2018). *Academic and student affairs educators make meaning of their collaboration on campus* (doctoral dissertation), University of Northern Colorado, Greeley, CO.

McClellan, G. S., Creager, K., & Savoca, M. (2018). *A good job: Campus employment as a high impact practice*. Sterling, VA: Stylus.

O'Connor, S., Levy, M. A., & Polnariev, B. A. (2016). Curricular infusion of student success strategies. In M. A. Levy & B. A. Polnariev (Eds.). *Academic and student affairs collaboration: Creating a culture of student success*. New York, NY: Routledge.

Reisinger, D. (2016, October 5). Remembering Steve Jobs: 5 year later. *Fortune*. Retrieved from http://fortune.com/2016/10/05/remembering-steve-jobs/

Seligson, A. (2015, April 29). An observation about the mission of higher education. [Blog post]. Public Purpose. Campus Compact.

Sherman, M., Edison, S., Rehberg, B., & Danoesastro, M. (2017, July 19). Taking agile way beyond software. [Blog post]. Retrieved from https://bcg.com/en-us/publications/2017/technology-digital-organization-taking-agile-way-beyond-software.aspx

Sigelman, M., Bittle, S., Markow, W., & Francis, B. (2019). *The hybrid job economy: How new skills are rewriting the DNA of the job market*. Boston, MA: Burning Glass Technologies.

"silo" (n.d.). *Oxford English Dictionary*. Retrieved January 12, 2019 from https://en.oxforddictionaries.com/definition/silo

Terenzini, P. T., Pascarella, E. T., & Blimling, G. (1999). Students' out-of-class experiences and their influences on learning and cognitive development: A literature review. *Journal of College Student Development, 40*(5), 610–623.

Tett, G. (2016). *The silo effect: The perils of expertise and the promise of breaking down barriers*. New York, NY: Simon & Schuster.

University of Maryland (n.d.). Honors College website.

University of Texas (n.d.). *Women in Natural Sciences Website*. Retrieved from https://cns.utexas.edu/wins

University of Wisconsin (n.d.). *Housing Website*. Retrieved from https://housing.wisc.edu/residence-halls/learning-communities/startup/100-hour-challenge/

Contributed Author

Marianna Savoca is assistant vice president of career development and experiential education at Stony Brook University where she leads campuswide initiatives to expand career-relevant, work-integrated learning experiences for undergraduate and graduate students. She is active professionally, now serving as president-elect of the National Society for Experiential Education. Dr. Savoca is also a faculty member in Higher Education Administration at Stony Brook and co-authored *A Good Job: Campus Employment as High Impact Practice* (Stylus, 2018). She earned a BS from SUNY Binghamton, MS from Indiana University, and a PhD in Higher Education Leadership from Colorado State University.

Kelley Bishop became director of the University of Maryland's career center in 2013. His 30-year background includes leading the career services operations at Michigan State University and Syracuse University, serving on the boards of the National Association of Colleges and Employers and the Walt Disney World College Program, and frequently consulting for other career centers. Kelley holds a Bachelor's degree in English Literature from Dartmouth College and a Master's degree in Counseling from Indiana University.

CHAPTER 7

Spartan-Ready at the University of Tampa

Tim Harding and Stephanie Russell Krebs

As indicated in Section 1, the T-model, which comprises depth of disciplinary knowledge and breadth of professional abilities (Gardner and Estry 2017), is important for all students regardless of academic major or career focus. Work-integrated learning (WIL), the practice of combining traditional academic study with student exposure to the world-of-work in their chosen profession, is widely considered instrumental in equipping new graduates with the required employability skills needed to function effectively in a work environment. As impactful as WIL is in showcasing depth and breadth of T-potential, it is not the only way to ensure students graduate with the ability to understand knowledge within or across systems, nor to interact meaningfully with diverse groups. Colleges need a comprehensive, institution-wide approach that infuses the T-model to create the broadest impact on most students.

Silos, as discussed by Savaco and Bishop (2019, this volume) in Chapter 6, have unfavorable implications for organizations, preventing communication, confusing roles and responsibilities, stifling expertise, wasting resources, and obstructing innovation and forward movement (Lemonedes 2018; Tett 2016). In higher education, silos are more typically an institutional norm, so finding a way to break them down to foster more open means of collaboration and partnership for collective student learning can be a significant challenge. Developing a sense of trust and common purpose is essential to move from a silo-focused to an institution-focused culture. Partnerships thrive when there are shared outcomes that help all constituents achieve their desired goals.

In 2011, an institution-wide competency development initiative, Spartan Ready™ was launched to support the career preparation of all University of Tampa (UT) students. While a natural inclination toward career preparation exists, the T-inspired Spartan Ready™ initiative is rooted in the liberal arts philosophy, embraced by many faculty, in preparing graduates for strong career decision-making, civically minded engagement, and life-long critical thought. Spartan Ready™ can also aid in retention and persistence providing students with increased relevance for their entire collegiate experience as it relates to their sense of purpose.

Spartan Ready™

UT defines Spartan Ready™ as "graduating students who are prepared to be successful individuals with an advanced understanding of their field of study, the interdisciplinary workplace and how to be leaders who contribute to society" (Harding 2011). Through the curriculum and cocurricular programming, UT focuses on developing students in seven high-demand competency areas: communication, interpersonal abilities, critical thinking, organization, global engagement, teamwork, and self-awareness, with a strong emphasis on the innovative, boundary spanning T-shaped professional. Competency development is essential for student success after graduation. Thus, like UT, many universities are now integrating some form of institution-wide competency development.

An institution-wide approach, such as Spartan Ready™, calls on all constituents to make a culture shift, which can bring synergy to pockets of similar learning that may be occurring across campus but in a disjointed way. Institutional initiatives can be challenging in higher education, the success of which requires a strategic approach that is inclusive of all campus stakeholders and external partners.

Mounting Evidence

At the same time UT was developing an institution-wide competency-based initiative, Clemson University was on a similar journey. Each institution took a different approach to competency implementation, yet both institutions experienced success in impacting the overall culture. As a result of these positive, campus-wide outcomes, the two institutions joined forces to design a nationwide forum on institution-wide, competency-based development and career readiness to elevate competency initiatives. In so doing, the staff from both institutions created a framework, composed of four competency pillars (Figure 7.1) upon which colleges and universities could create their own approach to institution-wide competency-based initiatives respectful of their uniqueness, institutional needs, and priorities.

Pillar 1 Conceptualization and Planning	Pillar 2 Coalition Building
Competency learning, development and articulation should be made apparent and infused into the curriculum and co-curriculum to provide opportunities for students to actively demonstrate competency development and readiness. Framing programs, services and one-on-one conversations around competencies provide students with multiple touchpoints throughout their time at the institution.	Institution-wide competency development and career readiness should be integrated broadly into the life and culture of the institution and their value should be reflected in institution/division/department stratefic plans and general education. A common vocabulary and definitions for the competencies will provide an institution-wide understanding and universal brand. One area may take the lead in implementation while refraining from solely owning the initiative.
Pillar 3 Resources	**Pillar 4** Assessment
Institution-wide competency infusion may be achieved through new and re-purposed single departmental programs and shared resources. It is imperative to keep a pulse on trends and issues impacting higher education and the evolving world to ensure an institution-wide competency development approach remains relevant.	Competency development should be assessed, measured and tracked in curricular and co-curricular experiences. Collecting outcomes data will help individual students realize developmental progress and instutions work toward continued improvement.

Figure 7.1 The four pillars of institution-wide competency development are foundational for a strategic approach to comprehensive infusion across the campus. They may be used in any type of institution and are non-sequential providing opportunity for simultaneous application

The competency initiative pillars—conceptualization and planning, coalition building, resources, and assessment—are designed to be four foundational points from which to build a customized approach to students' academic development and career readiness. The pillars should not be viewed as sequential, rather, offer a means to build initiatives that consider the unique strengths and opportunities of each institution. The competency pillars may also be used as a model for institution-wide initiatives even if they are not focused specifically on competency development.

Pillar One

Competency learning, development, and articulation should be made apparent and infused into the curriculum and cocurriculum to provide opportunities for students to actively demonstrate competency development and readiness. Framing programs, services, and one-on-one conversations around competencies provide students with multiple touchpoints throughout their time at the institution.

The first pillar stresses the philosophical importance of an infused curricular and co-curricular approach, which provides the greatest opportunity for student impact. A single department within an institution, whether academic or cocurricular, will not be able to reach all students. This pillar acknowledges that students will have unique collegiate experiences in which their paths will cross a variety of faculty and staff through which they learn to become—Spartan Ready™. With this comprehensive approach, an institution is more likely to have multiple touchpoint opportunities from matriculation through graduation, resulting in a better connection between learning outcomes and their future relevant short- and long-term application.

Multiple touchpoints may come from individual, cocurricular, or classroom experiences. These developmental experiences are more powerful when they are the result of a partnership. An example of an infused curricular and cocurricular approach comes out of the UT's Wellness Center. The Live Well UT program is primarily a student-led initiative that empowers the UT community to continually improve healthy individual and community behaviors and lifestyles. Live Well UT is based on a holistic well-being philosophy that addresses the community's dynamic need and all aspects of a balanced life by providing a wide array of services and education. What makes the program unique is the discipline-specific faculty advisor model, which ties student-learning outcomes to the university-designed, Spartan Ready™ competencies. Many of the initiatives provide credit-bearing internship opportunities, bridging academic and student affairs boundaries.

Another example in early implementation is the UT residential curriculum: Spartan Living. Historically, the term "curriculum" was only thought to represent classroom-based learning. Higher education has since evolved to recognize learning outside the classroom to include robust forms of co-curriculum "curriculum." Based on five of the Spartan Ready competencies—self-awareness, life skills, interpersonal abilities, teamwork, and global engagement—Spartan Living reinforces that students who reside on campus learn and grow through living independently, sharing a space, and executing self-management. Spartan Living engages students in intentional and sequenced learning experiences tailored around self-exploration, increased understanding of others and of their environment, and multicultural and diversity awareness, and how their footprint impacts their surroundings in multiple and varied ways.

Pillar Two

Institution-wide competency development and career readiness should be integrated broadly into the life and culture of the institution and their value should be reflected in institution/division/department strategic plans and general education. A common vocabulary and definitions for the competencies will provide an institution-wide understanding and universal brand. One area may take the lead in implementation while refraining from solely owning the initiative.

The second pillar focuses on the theoretical infusion of institution-wide initiatives. Institutions need a common and agreed upon language and vocabulary that clearly defines any initiative. Spartan Ready™ has a clearly stated definition and well-delineated competency pillars that provide context, a means to describe and communicate, which are all important components of *culture*. While an initiative may be championed by a single department or division, institutions should seek to develop allies, champions, and ambassadors from across the university and resist the perception of a single entity's ownership.

Identifying institution-wide priorities presents an opportunity to create cross-campus partnerships, simultaneously infusing the T-model into strategic planning. One such opportunity presented itself to UT via the Quality Enhancement Plan (QEP), required by the Southern Association of Colleges and Schools Commission on Colleges for Accreditation. The QEP must (1) include a process identifying key issues emerging from institutional assessment, (2) focus on learning outcomes and the environment supporting student learning and accomplishing the mission of the institution, (3) demonstrate institutional capability for the initiation, implementation, and completion of the QEP, (4) include broad-based involvement of institutional constituencies in the development and proposed implementation of the QEP, and (5) identify goals and a plan to assess their achievement.

The UT's QEP is *Learning by Doing: Inquiry Based Experiential Education*. The plan has a focus on learning through both research and internship experiential education. The Applied Learning Experiences (ALEX), however, are designed to be interdisciplinary group internships for three to six students with different academic majors. Local organizations are invited to participate in this T-approach to address and solve real-world problems, explore new programs or services, or enhance products. The interdisciplinary group of students approach the internship as a team that brings a perspective, research and solutions through the lens of their academic discipline while also learning from the perspective of others. A faculty member from each of the represented disciplines works with and mentors all the students providing a T-learning experience that they might not otherwise have experienced. This mentorship arrangement allows both the student and the organization to benefit from expert guidance as the project unfolds. At the end of the experience, the ALEX groups do a presentation on their internship and learning outcomes for the campus community.

Another opportunity to strategically infuse T-competencies is across departmental boundaries. For example, a steering committee chaired by faculty and student affairs are charting the strategic path to infuse Spartan Ready™. This committee provides the means to consider the intersection of students' learning in their collegiate experience both inside and outside of the classroom and explore the ways in which the institution can offer the most and best means to achieve T-student growth and competency development.

It would be easier to house a program like Spartan Ready™ in a career center, thinking of the competencies and T- model solely in the context of career development. While a home base is important, UT is intentional about having the initiative live broadly in the division of student affairs with a strong and purposeful tie to academic affairs. The Spartan Ready™ initiative is both grassroots up, developed and executed by our Associate Dean of Career Development and Engagement, and championed top-down from our President, Vice President for Student Affairs, and our Associate Dean of Teaching and Learning, as well as university senior leadership. In campus speeches by the President, Spartan Ready™ competencies have infiltrated our campus culture at all levels and is the common language of the university.

The Development and University Relations division provides the evidence of the level of campuswide strategic infusion. The latest UT capital campaign was recently launched bearing the name Spartan Ready™ Philanthropy, focusing on UT's mission to "develop the whole student—the professionalism and life skills needed to be their best, ready for success in life and in the workplace and leaders who contribute to society." The campaign literature highlights student narratives and interviews about their UT experience and postgraduate preparation to be Spartan Ready™.

Pillar Three

Institution-wide competency infusion may be achieved through new and re-purposed single departmental programs, collaborative initiatives, and shared resources. It is imperative to keep a pulse on trends and

issues impacting higher education and the evolving world to ensure an
institution-wide competency development approach remains relevant.

The third pillar is designed to consider operational aspects, which might include new programs but also challenge the campus community to rethink existing programs, classes, and services to align learning outcomes with the institution-wide initiative. It is very common for people to feel overwhelmed if it appears that they may be being asked to do what they perceive as more when their plate is already full. While there may be some new approaches that institutions will want to consider, those already in existence may just need some tweaks to align them with mapped learning to the institution-wide initiative. With an institution-wide initiative, there is also a greater opportunity for collaboration between departments and even between academic and co-curricular entities, which can result in enhanced student learning. It also provides a means to creatively share resources and provide a broader student impact.

An example of co-curricular infusion is UT's President's Leadership Fellows. The program is a four-year interdisciplinary cohort initiative based on the social change model for leadership (Astin and Astin 1996). Students learn about leadership, the Spartan Ready™ competencies, and apply their knowledge through a culminating social change project where the students can critically analyze, and problem solve through the lens of their major in concert with other academic disciplines and leadership theory thus providing a more holistic approach.

In addition, UT received a $250,000 grant from the TD Charitable Foundation to develop a co-curricular experience to better support first generation and underrepresented students who have significant unmet financial need. The grant enables eligible students who complete specific program requirements, which are behaviors known to contribute to overall student success, to receive additional financial support each semester over the course of four years, up to $10,000. In early-stage implementation, special consideration will be given to students from Puerto Rico and the Caribbean Islands who were displaced by Hurricane Maria. Based on student development research and UT's experience, the identified tasks, events, workshops, and activities will help the students, to be known as Crescent Scholars, achieve the following goals: (1) engage in academic behaviors which promote student success, (2) develop a financial readiness plan, (3) develop a personal career strategy, and (4) graduate in four years with completed Spartan-Ready curriculum and identified postgraduation career options.

The faculty are collaborating to create interdisciplinary classes. One such honors class, titled *The Politics of Water*, is a partnership of biology, sociology, and communication faculty who will explore the scientific research about unhealthy drinking water with the students while they also consider the varied impact on different socioeconomic groups. With this data and information, the class will design and implement an educational outreach plan considerate of the science and socioeconomic diversity. Students who might have only been previously exposed to the context of their major now can view the issues from a more comprehensive lens while reflecting on the competencies used in so doing.

Pillar Four

> *Competency development should be assessed, measured, and tracked in curricular and co-curricular experiences. Collecting outcomes data will help individual students realize developmental progress and institutions work toward continued improvement.*

The fourth pillar is both the most challenging and perhaps the highest priority. Whether the T-model is embedded in something like Spartan Ready™, stand alone, or infused in another institution-wide initiative, universities must assess related student learning and development. Competency-based initiatives can be assessed through micro- and macro-assessment practices. Micro-assessment provides data on individual growth while macro-assessment measures the overall institutional or programmatic success by aggregating students' learning outcomes. For example, assessing individual honor students on their academic achievement would be an example of micro-assessment because micro-assessment can demonstrate individual student T-development, whereas assessing students in an honors program against the rest of the student body would be an example of macro-assessment.

In 2016, the Division of Student Affairs adopted the Spartan Ready™ Competencies as the common learning domains for all functional areas. The Student Affairs Strategic Planning and Assessment team utilizes a common template that was adapted to incorporate the competencies. All student affairs areas measure yearly learning in the Spartan Ready™ competency domains. The team also offers departmental consultations to areas that are planning assessment projects to assist them in crafting assessment tools that match what they are intending to measure. From an integrated student learning report tied to the annual report, to a summer assessment showcase, to assessment spotlights, several methods have been employed with varying levels of success.

Perhaps the most challenging aspect of assessment is the need to aggregate the individual student learning achieved from the multiple touchpoints across the campus. Technology platforms are currently lagging though some products provide the means for students to gather artifacts and record experiences via online portfolios. One such product is badging, which is a means to credential or recognize a level of learning or achievement, has become a popular approach to assessment. Care should be taken, however, that badging is the culmination of assessed learning. Some tools merely track student participation in activities tagged as focused on learning but do not measure associated learning outcomes. This merely tracks student attendance and lacks verifiable evidence of students' learning.

A Unique Journey Versus a *Silver Bullet*

An institution-wide initiative that results in a culture shift should be viewed more as a journey than a one-time program implementation that will cause a sudden culture shift. It will be a long process, so the process should be dynamic, allowing many opportunities for feedback, input, and innovation with an eye to seeking active participation and initiative promotion from every corner of the institution.

While the focus of the competency-based pillars implementation at UT has mostly been on the institution, it is important to consider external stakeholders. Employers that recruit graduates and interns can play a key role. Alumni and students' parents may also be tapped to support this shift toward a T-graduate. Every institution is unique. While some best practices metioned in this chapter may be scaled and replicated at other institutions, more often than not they should be considered as a means of generating ideas while considering the unique nature of institutional context.

T-initiatives will thrive at an institution committed to campuswide cultural infusion, strategic integration in the mission, mapped learning from existing and new programs, and macro- and micro-assessment. Identifying and enlisting faculty, staff, and administrative champions is key to success.

References

Astin, A., & Astin, H. (1996). *A social change model of leadership.* Lansing, CA: University of California, Los Angeles and the Higher Education Research Institute.

Gardner, P., & Estry, D. (2017). *A primer on the T-professional. Lansing,* MI: Michigan State University and the Collegiate Employment Research Institute.

Harding, T. (2011). Spartan ready. Retrieved from http://ut.edu/spartanready/

Lemonedes, G. H. (2018). *Academic and student affairs educators make meaning of their collaboration on campus* (PhD). University of Northern Colorado, Greeley, CO.

Savoca, M., & Bishop, K. D. (2019). Academic and student affairs together: Breaking organizational Silos. In P. Gardner & H. N. Maietta (Eds.), *The T-professional model and undergraduate education: Advancing the talent development.* New York, NY: Business Expert Press.

Tett, G. (2016). *The silo effect: The perils of expertise and the promise of breaking down barriers.* New York, NY: Simon & Schuster.

Contributed Author

Tim Harding is the Associate Dean of Career Development and Engagement at The University of Tampa in Tampa, Florida, and has worked in higher education for over 25 years. Harding earned an M.S. in Education from Indiana University and a B.A. from Anderson University. Harding is a cofounder of the Competency Development Symposium and serves on the planning committee for the annual gathering. He served as President of the Southern Association of Colleges and Employers and the Career

Development Professionals of Indiana. He is on the Board of Directors for the National Association of Colleges and Employers.

Stephanie Russell Krebs is the Vice President for Student Affairs and Dean of Students for The University of Tampa. Dr. Krebs holds a bachelor's degree in theater/speech from Butler University (IN), a master's degree from Western Illinois University in college student personnel, and a doctorate from Colorado State University in higher education leadership. Dr. Krebs is a graduate of the Management Development Program at Harvard University and is a DiversityFIRST™ Certified Diversity Professional (CDP). Dr. Krebs' research interests include interfaith dialogue and work-life integration and has been published in the *NASPA (National Association of Student Personnel Administrators) Journal of College and Character* and the *NASPA Journal about Women in Higher Education.*

CHAPTER 8

Driving Purpose

Marcus Sanderlin

Purpose exploration and meaningful career navigation have become a focal point in higher education. With over 19 million students enrolled in U.S. colleges annually (National Center for Educational Statistics 2018), the demographic of collegegoers continues to diversify. Equally diverse are student expectations of the college experience. While students enter college with varying social, personal, and professional pressures and anticipations, a growing number enroll with the added hope of exploring who they are, learning about their passions, and preparing to transition as T-professionals into careers of meaning and purpose.

As Hunsacker and Rivera (2019, this volume) outline in Chapter 4, the intersection of the two axes of the T is the ME, or knowledge of the self. The ME is the most critical component of the T because it showcases how T-professionals are able to function effectively in the workplace and integrate components of student academic success and career development. If students are provided tools and resources to define, refine, and affirm their purpose, the ME of the T will become more well-rounded and fulfilled.

This chapter will provide strategies to empower students to more fully define their ME through purpose exploration and navigation. Three key pillars will be outlined for navigating this process: (1) defining purpose: shifting the perception of purpose to be attainable and relevant; (2) exploring purpose: leveraging reflective questioning and self-assessments to discharge the *why* behind the *what*; and (3) affirming purpose: unpacking curricular and cocurricular experiences to uncover meaningful connections.

Defining Purpose: Making the Idea of Purpose Seem Attainable and Relevant to Students

Purpose definition and mapping can be an overwhelming and strenuous process, especially for college students who are navigating a range of pressures, priorities, and developmental changes. At the center the T is the ME, which is composed of three overlapping domains of personal development: purpose, awareness, and confidence or PAC (Hunsacker and Rivera 2019). Cultivating one's purpose develops the ME and vice versa because they are interconnected.

William Damon (2009) defines purpose as "a stable and generalized intention to accomplish something that is at the same time meaningful to the self and consequential for the world beyond the self" (p. 33). By integrating the importance of internal meaning and external impact, this definition highlights the reality that purpose is primarily grounded in self-understanding and is further honed and developed by gained experience. Unfortunately for many students, there can be a disconnect between their perception of what it means to have purpose and their ability to articulate a definitive definition for their purpose.

The process of coaching students to define purpose initiates an awareness process connected directly to the ME. The process of coaching begins with a simple question, *what does it mean to have purpose?* This question allows for the student to take ownership of the conversation and establish a baseline as to what purpose is to them, how they view it, and the traits that reflect purpose at a high level.

Once the student is able to define what purpose is, and what it means to them, the next step is to ensure the student believes a sense of purpose is achievable. Lack of confidence (an underdeveloped ME) often stems from the ambiguity of what it looks like for someone to actually navigate toward their sense of purpose. The connection between aspiration and realization can be addressed by students investing in the process, but, more importantly, by the affirmation and environment created by the institution. Through fostering a sense of belonging and connection, a deeper level of trust emerges, which allows the student to be more open to exploring goals.

Exploring Purpose: Exploring the
Why Behind Your *What*

What is the *why* behind your *what*? As students enroll in college and navigate the higher education experience, they are told about and often focus on the *what* but seldom the *why*. *What* is my major? *What* do I have to do to graduate? *What* will I do when I graduate? Simon Sinek (2009) proposes the concept of starting with *why*, leveraging the *why* to serve as an incentive for people to take action. Students who can gain insights into the *why* make the *what* seem less like to-do's and more like *get to's*. The pivot to *why* challenges students to focus on the end goal, and then use the *what* as stepping stones and opportunities to prepare for and move closer toward the goal. Changing the order so that *why* guides student effort and actions is the catalyst that allows students to effectively realize and explore their sense of purpose.

Show and Prove: Exploring Who I Am

When defining purpose, William Damon (2009) draws attention to two key variables: (1) internal meaning and (2) external impact. Internal meaning references the importance for the student to identify and realize who they are at their core. External impact reflects the difference that an individual aspires to make in the world around them (Damon 2009). These two variables provide the framework for students to begin grappling with the idea of purpose. The exploration and navigation toward purpose challenges students to ask three primary questions: Who am I? What do I aspire to do? How do I want to make an impact in the world?

Formal and informal assessment tools such as the Strong Interest Inventory or the Myers-Briggs Type Indicator (MBTI) are available to coach students by identifying their skills, interests, and values. These tools leverage theory and data to relate insights about a student's ME to potential career options. Informal assessment techniques or exploratory questioning can also be leveraged to support students with realizing attributes like skills, interests, and values. Below are examples of questions that can be utilized to begin the exploring process:

- What are three skills that make you a strong contributor to a team?

- What do you like to learn about?
- What are three values you have that are nonnegotiable to you?
- If you could do anything and not fail, what would it be and why?

Answers to these questions may provide insight into one's purpose. Once identified, a student will be able to use these factors to "stress test" future decisions and options. Understanding their attributes allows for the affirming and reaffirming process to take place, utilizing this content to evaluate the fit of potential career options. For example, students who value family time and consistent work hours may find careers requiring high travel like consulting to be counter to those values. When navigating the path to purpose, the key focus should be keeping the student as the focal point of the conversation and prompting them to leverage reflection to guide their understanding and exploration. This can be done by challenging students to start with self-reflection, as they not only explore who they are, but how their skills, interests, and values inform their developing sense of purpose.

An example of starting with self-reflection as a means of exploration is seen in the Wake Forest University Ready7 Framework, which provides a seven-step model for strategically coaching students from self-awareness toward career and life readiness (Wake Forest University 2019). Using a seven-step process—(1) self-awareness, (2) career awareness, (3) personal branding, (4) networking and relationship building, (5) interviewing skills, (6) professional skills and literacy, and (7) life and leadership—Ready7 positions students at the center of their career journey. Students are not only able to articulate what they are interested in doing, but how their skills, interests, and values align with industry and job function. Moreover, this framework allows students to build connections between who they are, what they intend to do, and the impact (purpose) they aspire to have.

Articulating Purpose

The act of exploring purpose is hard, but articulating purpose is even more challenging. While identifying the intrinsic factors that encompass purpose, there is a need for students to craft language surrounding their purpose and future career aspirations. This awareness is central to the ME of the T in that one learns with and from others in order to fully gain an awareness of self. Like a student having a professional pitch, developing a purpose statement provides a framework for current and future aspirations. Questions that can support students in developing language to articulate their sense of purpose are:

- What does success look like to you?
- What is your why? What is the legacy that you hope to leave behind?
- How would you like to make an impact on the world?

Another resource that can be used in this effort is a Purpose Statement Activity. Inspired by Bill Johnson's *Meaningful Work* (Johnson 2015), the Purpose Statement Activity provides tangible language that students can use as they continue to explore and affirm their sense of purpose. The following statements provide a template to begin to articulate their sense of purpose:

- Because I value [*values*], I aspire to use my [*skills*], to *impact* [*what you want to offer the world*].
- Because I am interested in [*interests*], I will leverage my [*skills*], to *impact* [*what you want to offer the world*].

While these frameworks provide meaningful insights to all students, this intervention proved particularly impactful when used to support first generation and underserved students. At the Michigan State University, through cross-campus collaboration, opportunities were created for these particular populations to engage in self-exploration and purpose navigation. During career workshops hosted for incoming first-year students participating in college summer transition programs, the Purpose Statement Activity empowered students to explore their sense of purpose. At the conclusion of the workshop, every student had not only reflected on who they were (explored their ME), but also developed language surrounding how the ME informed the impact they aspired to have on the world. This intervention, especially when paired with the W.H.O. Action Plan discussed later in this chapter, provides a powerful foundation for empowering first generation and underserved students to leverage purpose as a compass to navigate their college experience.

Affirming Purpose: Unpacking Experiences to Uncover Meaningful Connections

An individual's ability to understand and articulate meaning from their gained experiences leads to a more clearly defined purpose. Similarly, a well-defined ME helps the individual effectively pursue these goals despite struggles and setbacks. Experience empowers students to affirm and reaffirm their views, beliefs, and expectations of future aspirations and opportunities. As students transition from exploring to affirming their sense of purpose, their gained experiences either support their career aspirations or challenge them to reassess their career trajectory. Such experiences may be acquired within the classroom, through cocurricular engagements, or via work or internship opportunities as detailed in Martin and Rees's (2019, this volume) forthcoming chapter. However, regardless of how or where the experience is generated, the importance of the engagement lies within the student's ability to identify and articulate the gained skills and boundary spanning competencies (Rowe and Drysdale, 2019 this volume).

While unpacking these opportunities, practitioners should inquire how the experiences (1) impacted the student personally/professionally and (2) either affirmed or challenged the student's future aspirations/sense of purpose? These questions challenge the student to recognize the impacts and gained knowledge from various experiences and then identify connections between either past experiences, current views, or future ambitions. During this stage in the purpose navigation process, it is also important for students to remember that not every experience is a job, but every job is an experience. Focusing on the *why* of the experience, less on, for instance, the job title, allows students to identify skills and competencies within any job, not just those that are directly related to their field of interest.

A tool for guiding students through the process of meaning-making is the Pursuit of Purpose Activity (Figure 8.1). The activity begins with a past, present, and future reflection prompted by a series of questions where students navigate a linear process to identify where they have been, where they currently are, and where they plan to go. The second phase of the activity challenges students to find meaning in their past experiences and create action steps toward the future. Through this process, they can practice affirming and reaffirming their goals and sense of purpose, which strengthening their ME.

The Pursuit of Purpose (Figure 8.1) activity also provides an effective framework to coach students through articulating how challenges and adversity can also offer valuable insight on their sense of self. At the Michigan State University, this activity was often utilized when coaching students on academic probation, challenging them to identify the factors that influenced their subpar academic performance and reconstruct their expectations for their college experience moving forward. The intervention prompted students to revisit their sense of purpose, unpack whether their gained experience either affirmed or challenged this goal, and develop future steps. Not only did the process allow for these students to gain a better sense of self, but also empowered them to own their experience, ignite their grit and show resilience to overcome challenges. As a result, these students reported having a clearer sense of purpose and greater awareness of strategies and resources to maximize the remainder of their college experience.

Pursuit of purpose

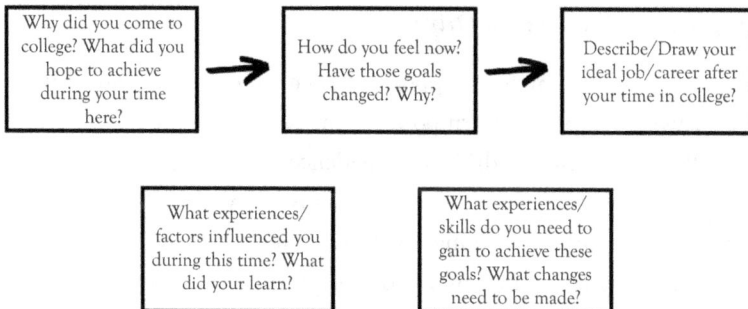

Figure 8.1 Pursuit of purpose activity

Source: Sanderlin 2019

Embracing the Process

As important as it is for students to define purpose, it is equally important for them to own the process of driving toward it. As students engage in the purpose exploration process, they must apply the effort needed to navigate through the process. Angela Duckworth (2016) speaks to effort counting twice, stating

talent × effort = skill; skill × effort = achievement

This formula outlined the process of moving from talent to achievement, wherein a person's effort proves foundational in their ability to demonstrate grit, exhibiting a combination of perseverance and passion toward a long-term goal (Duckworth 2016). Chickering and Reisser (1993) also propose that "developing purpose entails an increasing ability to be intentional, to assess interests and options, to clarify goals, to make plans, and to persist despite obstacles" (p. 209). As practitioners, it is important to acknowledge that for students to effectively navigate toward their purpose, it will come to them at a cost. Students who commit to the process of exploring and driving toward purpose will likely do so at the expense of effort, energy, and time. A question frequently posed to students regarding this concern is: *What are you willing to sacrifice to become the person you aspire to be?* A major alone is not purpose, and a job alone is not a career. However, if students use their college experience strategically, they can not only leave their respective institution with a next step, but more importantly, have a purpose-driven approach to their career trajectory.

Empowering Students to Drive

The most impactful way to support a student in exploring and realizing their sense of purpose is to empower them to own the process and allow them the opportunity to drive the experience. By setting actionable goals and creating a strategy for success, the onus is given to the students to continue the work of defining, exploring, and affirming their sense of purpose. One strategy that may prove helpful in this effort is a W.H.O. Action Plan.

Originally developed to support first-generation and underrepresented student populations with career exploration, the W.H.O. Action

Plan provides actionable steps for students as they navigate toward their sense of purpose:

W: What are three goals you have for this upcoming year to help you explore and move toward your purpose?

H: How do you plan to work toward and achieve these goals?

O: One campus resource and/or one faculty or staff that you are going to connect with to help you achieve these goals?

W.H.O. questions provide a platform for goal-setting, action steps, and support seeking. Not only are these skills vital toward purpose navigation, but they also embody the skills necessary for strategic thinking, problem solving, execution and collaboration, all ME attributes of the T-professional.

The Purposeful College Student

With a growing number of students entering college with the expectation of acquiring jobs with purpose and meaning, higher education professionals should be galvanized to integrate purpose navigation as a pillar of the college experience. This chapter provides strategies to empower students to more fully define their ME through purpose exploration and navigation. As students learn to drive their sense of purpose, they will be armed with the tools needed to thrive as future T-professionals.

The goal of college should not be to simply to get a job, but to begin a career of meaningful work. In essence, this is purpose. Purpose is about impact, displayed through the integration of skills, interests, and values into future opportunities. For this reason, it is imperative that students navigate toward purpose in a way that is grounded in who they are—in their ME. The process of *defining*, *exploring*, and *affirming* purpose—three critical components that comprise the ME of the T—provides an outline for coaching students through the process of leveraging self-understanding as a compass for future career navigation. Activating these three pillars creates a framework for students to develop into young professionals that enter the workplace with a deeper understanding of their self, awareness of their organizational value, with confidence to learn, engage, and make a positive impact in the world.

References

Chickering, A. W., & Reisser, L. (1993). *Education and identity.* (2nd ed). San Francisco, CA: Jossey-Bass.

Damon, W. (2009). *The path to purpose how young people find their calling in life.* New York, NY: Free Press.

Duckworth, A. (2016). *Grit: The power of passion and perseverance.* New York, NY: Scribner/Simon & Schuster.

Johnson, B. (2015). What is your meaningful work? *The Dream Dean.* Retrieved from https://thedreamdean.com/2015/07/24/your-meaningful-work-day-5-your-meaningful-work-statement/

National Center for Educational Statistics. (2018). Undergraduate enrollment. Retrieved from https://nces.ed.gov/programs/coe/indicator_cha.asp

Sinek, S. (2009). *Start with why: How great leaders inspire everyone to take action.* New York, NY: Portfolio.

Wake Forest University. (2019). *What it means to be Ready7.* Office of Personal and Career Development. Retrieved from https://opcd.wfu.edu/start-here/ready7/

Contributed Author

Marcus Sanderlin has a passion for empowering students to pursue meaningful careers centered around their sense of purpose. Sanderlin's work spans from coaching students to educating faculty and staff on strategies for purpose navigation and education. Sanderlin strives to infuse purpose into all aspects of the college experience. Marcus Sanderlin acquired his bachelor of science in elementary education from the University of Central Florida, and his master of arts in student affairs administration from the Michigan State University. He currently serves as an Associate Director of Market Readiness and Employment in the Wake Forest University School of Business.

CHAPTER 9

The Role of Work-Integrated Learning in Developing T-graduates

Andrew J. Martin and Malcolm Rees

The illustration that opens this volume showcases the T-professional as someone who has the professional abilities needed to interact with others of varying disciplines at the same time understanding how individuals with that knowledge function and collaborate to accomplish outcomes within or across systems (Gardner 2017). There is no greater occasion for individuals, particularly college students, to experience T-development than during work-integrated learning (WIL). WIL provides students with an opportunity to incorporate academic learning with professional experience and encourages both industry feedback on one's individual capability and offers an opportunity for self-reflection (Smith 2012). This chapter highlights the need for WIL in the context of building a stronger T-workforce and supports this assertion by highlighting student's reflections of WIL experiences from the sport management and coaching practicum at Massey University, New Zealand.

Understanding student's perceptions of their WIL experiences helps to inform and change teaching practice to focus on specific graduate needs, as well as offer faculty and supervising staff a broader understanding of ways in which WIL fosters enjoyment, achievement, and reinforces career decision-making (Martin and Rees 2019a; Usher 2012) by providing necessary exposure to relevant work settings. It is widely researched that WIL offers many benefits to the participant, including the development of personal attributes involving self-management, enterprise, and effective

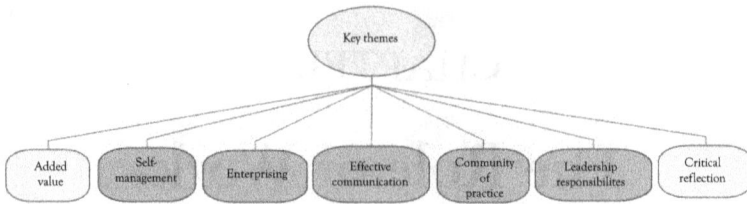

Figure 9.1 Key themes

Source: (Martin and Rees 2018)

communication (Haddara and Skanes 2007; Jackson and Wilton 2016; Smith 2012). In a study by Martin and Rees (2019a) on the benefits and added value of WIL on college students, professional development of a community of practice, leadership responsibilities, and critical reflection skills was also noted by respondents (Figure 9.1), which resonate with boundary crossing competencies of the horizontal bar of the T-model. Added value aspects of WIL relate to reinforcing employment decisions and enjoyment of their roles. These empirical findings also align closely with Fullan and Scott's (2014) six C's of deep learning: character, communication, creativity, citizenship, collaboration, and critical thinking.

Literature also reveals the following areas where WIL promotes positive career development: (1) the ability to self-assess work-related capabilities, (2) insight into the realities of a profession, (3) exposure to guidance and mentoring by established professionals, (4) enhanced confidence, and (5) career planning and networking. Obstructions to the career development process may include a lack of exposure to one's intended profession, inadequate mentoring and guidance, low self-esteem, and poor communication (Jackson and Wilton 2016).

Massey's WIL Experience

Whether empirical evidence supports the notion of the T-model, as developed through WIL experiences (Gardner and Estry 2017), is an area receiving much attention and research. The sport management and coaching program at Massey University, New Zealand requires all students to complete a practicum, which is a full-year course where students are based at a sport organization working on a specified project for a minimum of 180 hours. A learning contract is negotiated between the student, the supervisor within the organization and the academic supervisor responsible for coordinating the practicum at the university. This contract provides a detailed overview of the practicum, including expectations, responsibilities, and timeline (Martin 2013). Reflective practice is the primary pedagogy employed to integrate knowledge. Students keep a reflective journal composed of a brief synopsis (diary type format) outlining the duties performed, work reflections, and learning from all activities that take place throughout the practicum experience. The journal entails more than just listing experiences. It includes revisiting feelings and reevaluating the experience while linking theory to practice. Schön's notion of the "reflective practitioner" is particularly applicable to the WIL process. He argued that reflective practice is a learned skill most effectively introduced through an experiential component (Schön 1987; 1991).

Evaluating the WIL Experience

Understanding students' perceptions helps to inform and change teaching practice through increased focus on specific graduate attributes and a broader range of added value aspects of WIL programs. From the fall of 2007 to the spring of 2016, students ($n=299$) participated in the sport management practicum course at Massey University, New Zealand. In Martin and Rees's (2019a) case study, WIL student responses ($n=271$) from their final reflective journal entries, which all followed a similar structure, were examined in respect of their main tasks, perceived learning outcomes, and overall experiences from a work-based sports management practicum using thematic content analysis (TCA) (Braun and Clarke 2006). This content was coded in the first instance in a deductive manner against the five Massey University employability characteristics (enterprise, global citizenship, information literacy, self-management, and exercising leadership). If additional themes emerged from the coding analysis, this was also included in an inductive manner as new themes. The documents were not part of any course assessment but were initially collated to provide detail of practicum placements and learning outcomes for future students to reference. Students who participated in the practicum were enrolled in one of the following: Bachelor of Sport and

Exercise (58 percent; Major in Management and Coaching), Bachelor of Business Studies (36 percent; Major in Sport Business Management), or another qualification (6 percent).

Breadth and Depth

Findings from Martin and Rees (2019b) revealed the following T-professional breadth and depth themes delineated in Figure 9.2. Overall, there were 1,186 separate tasks or subtasks coded across all the participants from 2007 to 2016. The most frequent main task overall related to *organizing events* (71 percent) followed by *business activities* (21 percent), *coaching* (6 percent), and *team organization* (1.6 percent). A number of subtasks, both curricular and noncurricular in nature, were generated for two of the themes: *event organizing* and *business activities*. No such hierarchy emerged for either *coaching* or *team organization* (Figure 9.3). Example quotes are provided describing new skills and a practical understanding of what's required to succeed in the sport management industry.

> *This experience has given me a valuable opportunity to test my capabilities working in a sports industry setting. I have been involved in many different aspects of sport management where I have gained and found new skills. Time management has been a critical factor for staying on top of things; balancing work and personal life is so challenging.*

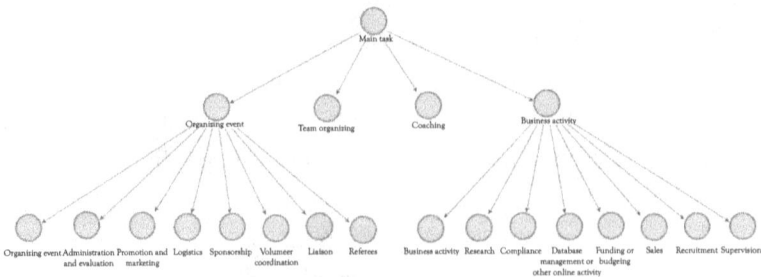

Figure 9.2 Thematic coding structure of students' main tasks in WIL

Source: (Martin and Rees 2019b)

Main tasks

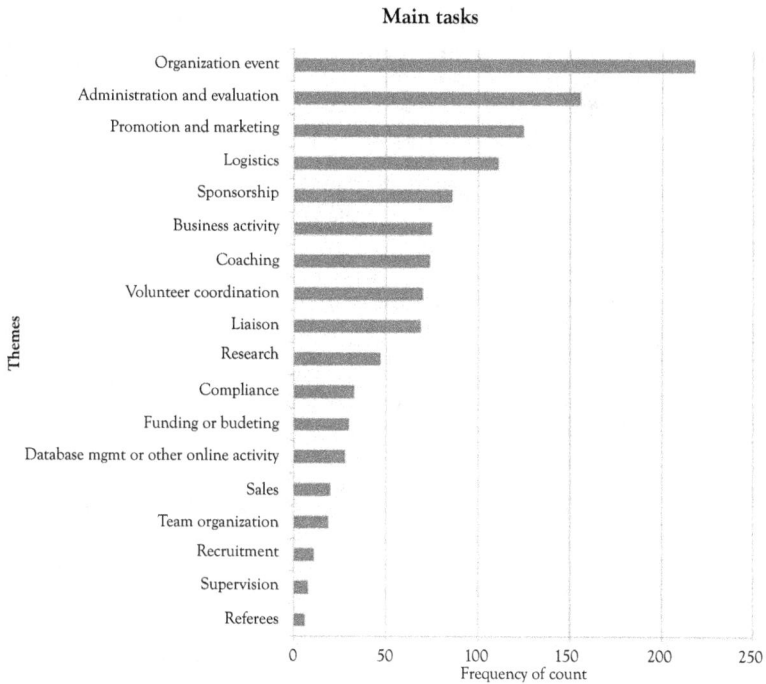

Figure 9.3 Main tasks, coding structure

Source: (Martin and Rees 2019b)

> *My experience has allowed me to get a practical understanding of what is required to be successful in sport management. The practicum allowed me to experience strategic planning, marketing, human resource management, and event management in a hard-working environment.*

Student feedback supports the development of the vertical columns of the T-model through the WIL experience. When you couple the activities undertaken with the graduate attributes that the students learned or experienced (Figure 9.1; Martin and Rees 2019b), their feedback is characterized by a depth of understanding of systems and disciplinary knowledge in at least one area (e.g., event management). The following comments illustrate this point:

> *"I have learned a lot about organizing an event and the need to pay attention to every detail when planning for an event."*

"I was able to gain a better understanding of what was involved in putting together a sports event, particularly of this size as there was a lot more to it than I first thought."

Students also reflected on developing a range of competencies and boundary spanning capabilities (e.g., across various business activities) through their WIL experience, which aligns with the horizontal rows of the T-model:

I have improved my understanding of areas such as promotion, marketing, publicity, and sponsorship.

My role was one that challenged me throughout. I have taken a great deal from my experiences; learning in, through and about a diverse range of managerial, promotional and leadership activities. The aforementioned includes human resource management, event management, risk management, contract management, and design projects.

Students highlighted learning from multiple tasks undertaken with different stakeholders, the range of responsibilities, and a variety of skills that have the potential to transfer to other disciplines and roles:

This practicum project will also be helpful to my previous workplace, because what I observed and experienced taught me a lot about how to be proactive and active every day. By doing simple exercises that dramatically cater and foster enjoyment, tasks completed, staff satisfaction, good and strong relationship and friendship between staff members and their managers.

I have also learned a lot about what it takes to start a project from scratch, such as how best to engage local organizations, including sporting groups; create a public presentation to share ideas, and how design concepts and funding options can affect the feasibility of a project.

These findings highlight that while skills are important, it is necessary to acknowledge the broader notions of career preparedness and enhancing employability. Results from this study and existing literature on similar WIL findings presented in this chapter do provide empirical support for the development of T-professionals who are cultivated through WIL experiences and are characterized by their deep disciplinary knowledge in at least one area, an understanding of systems, and their ability to function as *adaptive innovators* and cross boundaries between disciplines.

The Reflective Practitioner

The development of an effective *reflective practitioner* (Schön 1987; 1991) is through a cyclical experiential learning process (Kolb 1984) of *learning through reflection on doing* (Felicia 2011). Student feedback also highlighted that the reflective process encouraged critical, analytical, and systems thinking consistent with the T-model:

"Throughout my practicum experience, many difficulties arose. I was able to find a way to get around these difficulties by problem-solving and communicating."

One student reflected on the challenges of the practicum, but that perseverance provided longer-term support:

If I am being truly honest, the practicum on a personal level has been a struggle and very rarely enjoyable. Despite working in a sport I love, motivation has been hard to find throughout. However, I have strived to take all I can from the experience and sticking with it has provided me with the tools I will need in whatever career I choose to follow after this.

The value of applying theory to practice through the WIL process (Martin, Rees, Edwards, and Paku 2012) and the transfer of learning are reinforced by the following student insights:

I learned that throughout my time at university I have gained the theoretical knowledge required for a career in event management within the sports industry. I also believe I have the capability to manage other types of events. I have also learned that I am able to transfer this theoretical knowledge into practical work and event management planning.

I learned how to apply the knowledge in theory about sports management into practice first-hand. It has been a very enriching journey where I have learned to work on my strengths and improve on my weaknesses.

Development of Self

The development of self-efficacy has been highlighted as an important outcome in the process of WIL (Freudenberg, Cameron, and Brimble 2011; Reddan 2015; Subramaniam and Freudenberg 2007). In a broader sense, Bandura (1988) defined self-efficacy as a belief in one's ability to succeed in specific situations, which can play a major role on how one approaches goals, tasks, and challenges. Aspects of self-development were highlighted as the most common outcome of this current study. The following typical comments illustrate increased aspects of self-efficacy and the focus on self-development throughout the WIL experience, which is a catalyst for both personal and professional change and development.

I have learned a great deal about myself this year, not all of it has been positive, but the confidence I have gained in my public speaking, planning and time management have been invaluable and will put me in good stead for my move into the workforce and has definitely aided me in my development.

I found this [WIL] experience extremely beneficial to my development as an overall person. I have been able to progress in key areas such as communication, leadership, planning, and organization.

Conclusions and Implications

The findings of the WIL experiences from the sport management and coaching practicum at Massey University, New Zealand, indicate a breadth and depth of WIL activity. These findings reinforce the notion of developing T-professionals, who are characterized by their deep disciplinary knowledge in at least one area (e.g., event management), and their ability to function as *adaptive innovators* across boundaries between disciplines (e.g., various business activities). The findings also note that students' development as reflective practitioners require analytical, systems, and critical thinking to solve problems. These findings reinforce that successful project management involves the development of self-efficacy and boundary spanning competencies such as effective communication, organizational perspective and networks, as pointed out by Martin and Rees (2019b). The findings support the belief that the key aspects of the T-model can be cultivated through WIL experiences derived from a thematic content analysis (Braun and Clarke 2006) of student perceptions of their main tasks and overall learning experiences. From a teaching perspective, they also highlight the importance of a learning process that facilitates leadership and reflective work-based experiences to integrate theory and practice.

Acknowledgment

The research has been funded through the support of Ako Aotearoa, New Zealand, National Centre for Tertiary Teaching Excellence.

References

Bandura, A. (1988). Organizational application of social cognitive theory. *Australian Journal of Management, 13*(2), 275–302.

Braun, V., & Clarke, V. (2006). Using thematic analysis in psychology. *Qualitative Research in Psychology, 3*(2), 77–101.

Fullan, M., & Scott, G. (2014). *New pedagogies for deep learning whitepaper: Education PLUS the world will be led by people you can count on, including you!* Seattle, WA: Collaborative Impact SPC.

Felicia, P. (Ed.). (2011). *Handbook of research on improving learning and motivation through educational games: Multidisciplinary approaches: Multidisciplinary Approaches*. Hershey, PA: IGI Global.

Freudenberg, B., Cameron, C., & Brimble, M. (2011). The importance of self: Developing students' self-efficacy through work integrated learning. *The International Journal of Learning, 17*(10), 479–496.

Gardner, P., & Estry, D. W. (2017). Flourishing in the face of constant disruption: Cultivating the T-professional or adaptive innovator through WIL. In T. Bowan & M. Drysdale (Eds.), *Work Integrated Learning in the 21st century* (Volume 32, pp. 69–81). Bingley, UK: Emerald Publishing.

Jackson, D., & Wilton, N. (2016). Developing career management competencies among undergraduates and the role of work-integrated learning. *Teaching in Higher Education, 21*(3), 266–286.

Kolb, D. A. (1984). *Experiential learning: Experience as the source of learning and development*. Englewood Cliffs, NJ: Prentice Hall.

Martin, A. J. (2013). Reflections on 20 years of practicum, partnership and practice. *Asia Pacific Journal of Cooperative Education, 14*(3), 89–98.

Martin, A. J., & Rees, M. (2019a). Student insights: The added value of their WIL experiences. *International Journal of Work Integrated Learning, 20*(2), 189-199.

Martin, A. J., & Rees, M. (2019b). Student insights: *Developing T-shaped professionals through WIL*. *International Journal of Work Integrated Learning, 20(4)* (in press)

Martin, A. J., & Rees, M. (2018). *WIL outcomes: More than graduate attributes and employability?* Wellington: Ako Aotearoa.

Martin, A. J., Rees, M., Edwards, M., & Paku, L. (2012). An organisational overview of pedagogical practice in work integrated learning. *Asia Pacific Journal of Cooperative Education, 13*(1), 23–37.

Haddara, M., & Skanes, H. (2007). A reflection on cooperative education: from experience to experiential learning. *Asia-Pacific Journal of Cooperative Education, 8*(1), 67–6.

Reddan, G. (2015). Enhancing students' self-efficacy in making positive career decisions. *Asia-Pacific Journal of Cooperative Education, 16*(4), 291–300.

Richards, L. (2015). *Handling qualitative data: A practical guide* (3rd ed.), London: Sage.

Schön, D. A. (1991). *The reflective practitioner: How professionals think in action*. Aldershot, Hants: Arena.

Schön, D. A. (1987). *Educating the reflective practitioner: Toward a new design for teaching and learning in the professions*. San Francisco, CA: Jossey-Bass.

Smith, C. (2012). Evaluating the quality of work-integrated learning curricula: A comprehensive framework. *Higher Education Research and Development, 31*(2), 247–262.

Subramaniam, N., & Freudenberg, B. (2007). Preparing accounting students for success in the professional environment: enhancing self-efficacy through a work integrated learning program. *Asia-Pacific Journal of Cooperative Education, 8*(1), 87–102.

Usher, A. (2012). Measuring work-integrated learning: The development of the meta-competency test. *Journal of Cooperative Education and Internships, 46*(1), 5–15.

Contributed Author

Andrew J. Martin, Ph.D., is a Professor in the School of Sport, Exercise and Nutrition at Massey University, Palmerston North, New Zealand. He has been involved in a range of experiential learning projects in sport management education, coach education, and outdoor education. For more than 20 years, he has led the undergraduate professional preparation program in sport management for both internal and distance education students.

Malcolm Rees is the Manager of the Student Survey and Evaluation Unit, Massey University, Palmerston North, New Zealand. The Student Engagement and Evaluation Unit is a small team of evaluators and analysts with a responsibility for reviewing a variety of teaching and learning activities and other data gathering. Malcolm has been involved in several projects relating to Work Integrated Learning and is currently a certified NVivo Expert.

CHAPTER 10

Creating and Engaging T-engineers Inside and Outside of the Classroom

Denise Simmons

Inclusive T-competencies

A well-prepared engineering workforce is necessary to form and collaborate in interdependent relationships, manage multiple innovation projects, and adapt to changes in industry and stakeholder needs. From employers to accrediting bodies and professional societies, entities describe the competencies (i.e., knowledge, skills, and attitudes) they believe postsecondary engineering graduates should possess (ASEE 2013). While there are many ways to define these necessary competencies, the National Academy of Engineering (NAE) provides an enduring and inclusive definition of T-engineers. The Engineer of 2020 (E2020), an initiative of NAE's Committee on Engineering Education (CEE), presents facts, forecasts future conditions, and develops future scenarios of possible world conditions for 2020 engineers. The resulting 10 attributes—inclusive of T-competencies—are the attributes engineers must have by the year 2020 and beyond to prepare them to address world conditions (NAE 2004):

1. Strong analytical skills
2. Practical ingenuity (e.g., identifies problems and finds solutions through planning, combining, and adapting)
3. Creativity (e.g., invention, innovation, thinking outside the box, art)
4. Communication skills

5. Principles of business management
6. Principles of leadership
7. High ethical standards
8. Strong sense of professionalism
9. Dynamism, agility, resilience, flexibility (e.g., the ability to learn new things quickly and the ability to apply knowledge to new problems and new contexts)
10. Lifelong learning

While strong analytical skills are connected to depth in a specific engineering discipline, the other nine attributes are more related to broader, boundary spanning knowledge, skills, and attitudes. The question is how will engineering students gain these competencies while in college?

T-competencies and Out-of-Class Activities

National attention is focused on the quality of the undergraduate experience (NAS 2016). Supported by programs such as the National Science Foundation's Revolutionizing Engineering Departments (RED), many institutions are transforming engineering to better serve students (IUSE/ PFE: RED 2019). RED supports a revolutionary and sustainable change in the culture of engineering departments to produce new patterns of behavior or modes of operation. Program faculty and students will be better able to meet the changing workforce and societal needs ahead of us. The college experience comprises the formal and informal activities a student undertakes, including degree requirements and participation in cocurricular activities. While the student's disciplinary education centers on a specific field, the entire college experience is broader and more dynamic in the construction of the whole individual. This rounded experience comprises the breadth and depth that leads to development of a T-engineering professional. The cocurricular activities may not appear on a student's transcript but offer the critical opportunities to gain boundary spanning knowledge, skills, and attitudes.

Undergraduate students spend only 7.7 percent of their waking hours in formal, classroom settings (National Research Council 2009), leaving them in control of the remaining 92.3 percent of their time. Many students join clubs and organizations, play sports, work, participate in study abroad programs, complete internships, or join community groups. The academic experience does not consist of isolated activities in various buildings on campus but is rather supported and extended through participation in an array of out-of-class activities. Researchers have and continue to explore how these activities promote or hinder student engagement (Pascarella and Terenzini 2005; Zehner 2011; Simmons, Ye, Ohland, and Garahan 2018).

The term *out-of-class activity* is used to refer to any organized activity a student engages in during waking hours outside of formal instruction in a classroom. These typically involve one of three types: (1) curricular-related, (2) cocurricular, or (3) extracurricular activities. Curricular-related activities, often directly connected to an academic course, occur outside of class time while cocurricular activities, although not linked to an academic course, are designed with an educational lens. Extracurricular activities, on the other hand, capture activities that are not directly or indirectly connected to the academic curriculum. Table 10.1 (adapted from Simmons, Creamer, and Yu 2017) categorizes activities as either in-class or out-of-class based on their descriptions.

Table 10.1 Types of out-of-class activities

Activity Type	Description	Examples
Curricular-related	Tasks or activities associated with a course and connected to academic learning, but occurring outside of the classroom	Homework assignments, studying for an exam, group projects
Cocurricular	Activities, programs, and learning experiences that complement formal course content and/or degree major, but are not connected directly to a particular course	Engineering professional societies, undergraduate research, internships and co-ops
Extracurricular	Organizations or activities not explicitly connected to academic learning or the scope of a regular curriculum and usually carry no academic credit	Athletics (intercollegiate and intramural), fraternities and sororities, student government, job (off-campus or on-campus)

© From the Institute for STEM Education and Research 2017.

Since we know involvement in out-of-class activities contributes to the development of T-engineers, the question remains *How is this facilitated?*

T-development Through Faculty Engagement and Structured Leadership

Astin's theory of student involvement (1984) defines student involvement as the amount of physical and psychological energy a student allocates to the academic experience. This theory argues that simply exposing students to course material may not be enough to achieve academic success, but rather students must devote a sufficient amount of effort and energy to their total education experience to bring about desired outcomes. Additionally, it emphasizes students playing an active role in the learning process (Astin 1984). Thus, it can be argued that engineering students who do focus effort and energy to out-of-class engagement will have higher levels of T-development than their peers with no out-of-class involvement. While this chapter's focus does not aim to prove or disprove this argument, it does seek to use Astin's link between engagement and positive student educational outcomes to discuss implications for the curriculum and overall college experience of engineering students.

Given the vast array of out-of-class activities accessible to students, it is implausible to highlight every activity that produces T-competencies and offer curricular implications. Therefore, the remainder of this chapter will highlight two: (1) interaction with faculty and (2) student leadership.

Interaction with Faculty

Student interaction with faculty leads to improved student GPA and higher persistence and degree completion (Umbach and Wawrzynski 2005; Tierney, Colyar, and Corwin 2003; Hazeur 2008). Student interaction with faculty through different forms of engagement gives students agency to actively shape their education experience rather than being passive participants (Pepper 2009). According to Umbach and Wawrzynski (2005), "Students report higher levels of engagement and learning at institutions where faculty members use active and collaborative learning techniques, engage students in experiences, emphasize higher-order cognitive activities in the classroom, interact with students, challenge students academically, and value enriching educational experiences" (p. 153). Faculty assist students in socializing into the college culture (Hunsu, Simmons, Brown, and Adesope 2018).

Faculty members should be encouraged to create a dynamic, engaging learning environment in the classroom and extend themselves beyond the classroom. Based on experiences facilitating such courses, reviewing the existing frameworks and models, and analyzing effective practices for the design of learning environments and interventions in out-of-class activities, the Building Undergraduate Interventions for Learning and Development (BUILD) model (Simmons and Groen 2018) was developed. The BUILD model outlines three main components for educators to consider in the design of out-of-class interventions for undergraduate engineering students. These components include: (1) the learning environment, (2) structure, and (3) institutional support. In an out-of-class opportunity, students seek out and interact with faculty to help them develop social and cultural awareness. One example in creating such a learning environment was in a construction project management course where the comprehensive project required the students to investigate community need in the Dominican Republic. Factors such as design, schedule, and cost estimating a project, which met at least one need, were considered. Students then defended the results to a group of stakeholders that included potential investors. Students participated in field trips throughout the community, and discussions with community members and building officials outside of the class as part of the project development process. The course sought to help students develop:

- An awareness and understanding of the interrelationships among the self and professional responsibilities of an engineer, the communities, and existing infrastructure needs
- The ability to engage and learn from perspectives and experiences different from their own
- The capacity to adopt knowledge and skills gained through course readings and personal experiences to real-life problem-solving both alone and with others

- Curiosity to respectfully learn about the cultural diversity of other people, and on an individual level to traverse cultural boundaries to bridge differences and collaboratively reach common goals.

Unprompted observations of students pooled their previous experiences with community involvement and construction to help teams develop their project. Through listening to group conversations and reading reflective blog posts, instructors tracked their emerging awareness of the unique local needs and how their self and social awareness shaped their design. By the end of the course, the students were able to comparatively analyze their cultural and professional norms with those in the Dominican Republic and develop a perspective on ethical issues, professional practices, and construction methods that differed from the United States. The culminating experience showed students demonstrated gains in 8 of 10 inclusive T-competencies. This and countless examples of faculty involvement in classroom and out-of-class activities exist that produce positive social and cultural awareness. High levels of faculty engagement were also shown to promote student engagement and therefore the development of T-engineers (Simmons and Groen 2018).

Hierarchical Structure: Leadership Opportunities

When students build their leadership abilities, they receive more positive academic outcomes compared to students with no leadership experience (Pepper 2009). In addition, leadership development is directly linked to involvement in out-of-class activities (Astin 1993; Baxter Magolda 1992; Pascarella and Terenzini 2005; Burt et al. 2011); however, while overall involvement is highlighted, these studies fail to extricate what specific out-of-class activities promote the development of leadership qualities.

Promising research by Coffman (2012) reveals activities that provide hierarchical structures may promote leadership qualities more so than out-of-class activities where a hierarchical structure does not often exist. One example of a hierarchical leadership structure is student government, which offers the opportunity to hold numerous leadership positions (President, Treasurer, Committee Chair) within one organization. Hierarchical structures have clear and defined leadership roles, involvement of which is not solely focused on joining a hierarchical structured activity, but rather the process of obtaining and fulfilling the leadership role itself. Faculty are critical to this process by raising awareness of leadership competencies, soliciting input from employers, and incorporating hierarchical structures in their classroom (Groen, Simmons, and Clegorne 2018; Clegorne and Simmons 2018, 2017). One example is in the way teams are organized and roles formalized. Having a rotating project manager, for instance, provides an opportunity for each student to gain leadership experience.

Mitigating or Removing Barriers to Participating in Out-of-Class Activities

Involvement in out-of-class activities complements T-development for undergraduate engineering students. Despite the value of out-of-class engagement, students in engineering spend significantly more time preparing for class compared to their nonengineering counterparts, leaving less time for out-of-class activities (Lichtenstein, McCormick, Sheppard, and Puma 2010). Factors that reduce out-of-class participation are off-campus work, lack of activity knowledge, activity cost, family commitments, and demands of academic life (Tan and Pope 2007; VanZile-Tamsen and Bissonnette 2008; Yu and Simmons 2015; Simmons et al. 2018).

Implications for Lack of Participation

Out-of-class activities must be accessible to engineering students as a path to developing T-competencies demanded by the workforce and avoid further marginalization of certain groups. Students who have to work for pay and have family obligations are typically nontraditional, first-generation college students, students from low-income families, or racial and ethnic groups (Engle and Tinto 2008), and this is an area of opportunity for future research on how to allow this demographic access to participate in out-of-class activities. Such students can be surveyed to understand what types of accommodations they need. Additionally, all students can benefit from the T-enhancing strategies discussed in the Interaction with Faculty section of this chapter.

One outcome of the many engineering programs seeking to achieve a 120–125 credit hour curriculum is an intense focus on deep technical competencies 'hindering access, thus" making participation in out-of-class activities a necessity to develop T-engineers. In such programs, engineering students must be advised about the benefits of out-of-class activities to have a balanced and flourishing college experience while developing as a T-engineer. When students are educated on the benefits of participating in out-of-class activities and encouraged by faculty and staff to take advantage of these experiences, they will be more apt to engage early and often.

Conclusion

Although early research in understanding the relationship between out-of-class involvement and developing T-engineers is promising, more research is needed to fully realize the benefits of this involvement to developing workforce ready T-engineers. Unfortunately, little research has explored what specific elements of out-of-class activities produces deep and broad T-competencies and what the implications are for engineering curriculum development and shaping the college experience for engineering students should they lack these experiences. Engineering students expend a great deal of physical and psychological energies in academic coursework. Out-of-class involvement augments students' in-class experiences, providing occasion to become socialized into the institutional culture of the engineering department and university, and more importantly, to develop T-competencies. Strategies should be implemented to ensure out-of-class activities are accessible to students who have obligations outside of the university. Engineering programs may consider including such activities not necessarily or directly related to engineering in their recruitment messages to emphasize opportunities for intensive training for the engineering workforce while achieving a well-rounded educational experience. After more research on the complex relationship between out-of-class involvement and the T-engineering student is conducted, a clearer picture can be defined as to how out-of-class engagement can and should augment the formal curriculum.

Acknowledgment

The author gratefully acknowledges the National Science Foundation for supporting this work under CAREER grant no. EEC-1351156. Any opinions, findings, conclusions, or recommendations expressed here are those of the author and do not necessarily reflect the views of the National Science Foundation.

References

American Society of Engineering Education. (2013). *Transforming undergraduate education of engineers—phase 1: Synthesizing and integrating industry perspectives*. Washington, DC: American Society of Engineering Education.

Astin, A. (1984). Student involvement: A developmental theory for higher education. *Journal of College Student Personnel, 25*(4), 297–308.

Astin, A. (1993). *What matters in college: Four critical years revisited.* San Francisco, CA: Jossey-Bass.

Baxter Magolda, M. B. (1992). *Knowing and reasoning in college: Gender-related patterns in students' intellectual development.* San Francisco, CA: Jossey-Bass.

Burt, B., Carpenter, D., Finelli, C., Harding, T., Sutkus, J., Holsapple, M., … Ra, E. (2011). *Outcomes of engaging engineering undergraduates in co-curricular experiences.* Paper presented at the American Society for Engineering Education Annual Conference and Exposition, Vancouver, Canada. Retrieved from https://peer.asee.org/18498

Clegorne, N. A., & Simmons, D. R. (2017). *Engineering the best of both worlds: Towards a college curriculum of engaged citizen leadership for emerging engineers.* Proceedings of the Association for the Study of Higher Education Annual Conference, Houston, TX.

Clegorne, N. A., & Simmons, D. R. (2018). *Engineering professionalism: Towards a curricular model for professional skill and leadership competencies for emerging engineers.* Accepted for presentation at the Annual American Educational Research Association Conference, New York, NY.

Coffman, N. W. (2012). *An exploration of high school co-curricular activities.* University of Pennsylvania, ProQuest, UMI Dissertations Publishing.

Engle, J., & Tinto, V. (2008). *Moving beyond access: College success For low-income.* Washington, DC: The Pell Institute.

Groen, C. J., Simmons, D. R., & Clegorne, N. A. (2018). *Faculty ways of knowing, valuing and assessing leadership in the undergraduate engineering curriculum.* Proceedings of the 2018 American Society for Engineering Education Annual

Conference and Exposition, Salt Lake City, UT. Retrieved from https://peer.asee.org/30513

Hazeur, C. (2008). *Purposeful co-curricular activities designed to increase engagement: A practice brief based on BEAMS project outcomes.* Washington, DC: Institute for Higher Education Policy.

Hunsu, N., Simmons, D. R., Brown, S., & Adesope, O. O. (2018). *Developing an instrument of classroom social engagement.* Proceedings of the 2018 American Society for Engineering Education Annual Conference and Exposition, Salt Lake City, UT. Retrieved from https://peer.asee.org/30298

IUSE/Professional formation of engineers: Revolutionizing engineering departments (IUSE/PFE: RED). (2019, May 16). *National Science Foundation.* Retrieved from https://nsf.gov/funding/pgm_summ.jsp?pims_id=505105

Lichtenstein, G., McCormick, A. C., Sheppard, S. D., & Puma, J. (2010). Comparing the undergraduate experience of engineers to all other majors: Significant differences are programmatic. *Journal of Engineering Education,* 99(4), 305–317. https://doi.org/10.1002/j.2168-9830.2010.tb01065.x

National Academy of Engineering. (2004). *The engineer of 2020: Visions of engineering in the new century.* Washington, DC: The National Academies Press.

National Research Council. (2009). *Learning science in informal environments: People, places, and pursuits.* Washington, DC: National Academies Press.

Pascarella, E. T., & Terenzini, P. T. (2005). *How college affects students: A third decade of research* (Vol. 2). San Francisco, CA: Jossey-Bass.

Pepper, R. C. (2009). *The impact of motivation to lead on college students' cocurricular involvement.* Virginia Beach: ProQuest LLC, ProQuest, UMI Dissertations Publishing.

Simmons, D. R., & Groen, C. J. P. (2018). *Increasing impact of the hidden curriculum: Exploring student outcomes from out-of-class activities.* Proceedings of the 2018 American Society for Engineering Education Annual Conference and Exposition, Salt Lake City, UT. Retrieved from https://peer.asee.org/29935

Simmons, D. R., Creamer, E. G., & Yu, R.G. (2017). Involvement in out-of-class activities: A mixed research synthesis examining outcomes with a focus on engineering students. *Journal of STEM Education: Innovations and Research,* 18(2), 10–16.

Simmons, D. R., Ye, Y., Ohland, M. W., & Garahan, K. G. (2018). Understanding students' incentives for and barriers to out-of-class participation: profile of civil engineering student engagement. *Journal of Professional Issues in Engineering Education and Practice,* 144(2), 04017015. doi:10.1061/(ASCE) EI.1943-5541.0000353

Tan, D., & Pope, M. (2007). Participation in co-curricular activities: Nontraditional student perspectives. *College and University, 83*(1), 2–11.

Tierney, W., Colyar, J., & Corwin, Z. (2003). *Preparing for college: Building expectations, changing realities.* Los Angeles, CA: Center for Higher Education Policy Analysis.

Umbach, P., & Wawrzynski, M. (2005). Faculty do matter: The role of college faculty in student learning and engagement. *Research in Higher Education, 46*(2), 153–184.

VanZile-Tamsen, C., & Bissonnette, K. (2008). *Encouraging participation in enriching educational experiences – co-curricular activities and community service.* https://buffalo.edu/content/dam/www/provost/files/APBE/Briefs/Student-Experiences/EnrichingEducationalActivitiesI.pdf

Yu, R., & Simmons, D. R. (2015). *Synthesis of engineering undergraduate students' out of class involvement.* Proceedings of the 2015 American Society for Engineering Education Annual Conference and Exposition, Seattle, WA. doi:10.18260/p.24787

Zehner, A. (2011). *Co-curricular activities & student learning outcomes.* West Lafayette, IN: Purdue University.

Contributed Author

Denise R. Simmons, Ph.D., PE, LEED-AP, is an associate professor in the Department of Civil and Coastal Engineering in the Herbert Wertheim College of Engineering at the University of Florida. She holds a B.S., M.S., and Ph.D. in civil engineering and a graduate certificate in engineering education—all from Clemson University. She has over ten years of construction and civil engineering experience working for energy companies and as a project management consultant. Her integrated research, teaching and service goal is to be a thought leader in the professional formation of civil engineers, with a specific focus on project managers and the practical strategies that transform and sustain inclusive and productive organizations. Dr. Simmons' research is supported by awards from NSF including a CAREER award. She oversees the Simmons Research Lab (www.denisersimmons.com).

CHAPTER 11

The HEROIC Narrative Assessment System: Helping Undergrads Navigate Transitions

Rich Feller and Mark Franklin

Oh, the Places You'll Go! Dr. Seuss's (Geisel 1960) inspiration permeates graduation ceremonies with the promise of aligning new graduate talent with postgraduate opportunities. Yet undergraduates' internal voices ask, *Am I ready for what's next, let alone a lifetime of transitions?* With careers becoming more globalized, digitized and collaborative, "for too many people, the pathways, or as one expert puts it, the 'grooves toward careers' aren't as clear or accessible as they could be—or once were" (*The Chronicle of Higher Education* 2019, p. 6). A career planning system that supports holistic development, critical thinking, structured reflection of life stories and experiences, and employability over a lifetime is needed.

Maximizing the undergraduate experience to produce what Gardner and Estry (2017) describe as a T-professional capable "in multiple contexts, getting them to learn how to learn and how to utilize the information that you have, and being able to converse with a wide range of people" (*The Chronicle of Higher Education* 2017, p. 40) is essential. This chapter will introduce a career development system that promotes a HEROIC mindset, embracing filters of Hope, self-Efficacy, Resilience, Optimism, Intentional exploration, Curiosity and Clarity. Embedding a HEROIC Narrative Assessment System (HNAS) into the curricular framework of the undergraduate experience holds great potential for producing T-professionals sought by employers for jobs yet to be created.

Continuous learning, the ability to empathize and communicate across boundaries, agility, and sense making (Feller and Whichard 2005) are important career mobility keys and components of the T (Gardner and Estry 2017). The authors of *Career Ready Education* (*Chronicle of Higher Education* 2019) advocate it's time to move "beyond definitions of the skills gap and the accompanying blame game to the shifts that will push colleges to rethink their role" (p. 6). As innovation and intentional use of technology, time, space, and context to design personalized learning experiences grow, reflection on experience, clarifying assets and intentions, and creating narratives around possibilities can help undergrads present their desires to advisors, select career pathways, and translate skills and attributes to employers.

Having true depth and breadth as outlined in the T-model—deep knowledge combined with skills, competencies, and attitudes—requires students to make sense of how their learning and experience comes together, shape their goals, and conveys a personal story through reflective integration. This chapter presents the HEROIC Narrative Assessment System (HNAS), an exploration that guides users through a narrative career and life clarification process rooted in life stories, directed exploration of promising occupational possibilities, and the integration of experiences into a holistic picture. An explanation of the system's framework, descriptions of the personal discovery game *Who You Are Matters!* (WHAM), and *Online Storyteller* (Franklin and Feller 2014) offer opportunities to develop critical attributes and patterns promoted within the T-model (Gardner and Esty 2017).

Stability and Change Require a New Career Development System

Career and life roles go through cycles of stability and change as few adhere to a linear *Three Boxes of Life* (Bolles 1978) work and life planning model. Narrative assessment and meaning making through storytelling help create self-advocating learners with HEROIC mindsets (Feller 2017) that prepare them to embrace technological change and stand ready to learn boundary crossing competencies. A mindset of hope, self-efficacy, resiliency, optimism, intentional exploration, and curiosity help students develop a deeper knowledge of the systems, skills, and abilities needed to work within and across disciplines. This agility supports powerful learning that comes through failure, and understanding the perspectives of others essential to navigate transitions over a lifetime.

The HNAS leads users through a narrative career and life clarification process rooted in their life stories, followed by a guided exploration of promising occupational possibilities. The HNAS bridges the latest career theory and thinking with a framework (Figure 11.1) whose results indicate clear, confident, well-informed decisions by students. The HNAS is the foundation for creation of the *WYAM* and the *Online Storyteller* used throughout North America. Outcome research (Franklin, Yanar, and Feller 2015) within a private career management practice of 68 participants of various educational and professional backgrounds who completed at least four sessions found significant increases in hope, efficacy (confidence), resilience, and optimism (abbreviated as HERO) and collectively known as psychological capital (Luthans et al. 2007). Outcome study increases in HERO were correlated with increases in four key measures: clarity, career and life satisfaction, person–job fit, and employment status. Together these results support the HNAS as an evidence-based practice useful to help students thrive where adapting to innovation and boundary spanning are keys to success.

The University of Colorado at Boulder surveyed freshman, prebusiness students who engaged with in the *WYAM* personal discovery game as a required class activity and found that 71 percent indicated they agreed or strongly agreed that participating in the game was valuable, 85 percent indicated that they were moderately or extremely motivated to explore their career path as a result of the game play.

The University of Toronto OPTIONS Program supports Ph.D. students and postdoctoral fellows in exploring diverse career options with an emphasis on nonacademic possibilities. Participants learn career management within an 11-week, noncredit program facilitated by faculty and professional development experts. Participants reflect on strengths, desires, interests, and personal qualities using the *WYAM* game and *Online Storyteller*, to formulate a career exploration plan. They practice communicating skills and experiences, and learn about networking tools and labor market resources to identify and clarify career aspirations. Among the University of Toronto OPTIONS participants, 92 percent rated the HNAS's based *Online Storyteller* as *very useful* or *useful*, and using the same measure, ratings were 96 percent for *Creating a Career Statement* within the *WYAM* game. Participants rated the program 4.5 out of 5 consistently offering feedback on how powerfully the exploration exercises helped them generate career options, gain clarity, learn career management skills, and take action. Simon Fraser University reported the HNAS was "used successfully with students from first semester to those wrapping up a PhD in improved intentionality around their university experience" (Botelho 2019). In short, HERO helped students gain clarity, career options, a greater understanding of person–job fit. These evidence-based practices are useful to help students positively contribute and thrive in innovation and boundary spanning environments.

Charting educational pathways to careers faces a great paradox. Job seekers, college leaders, and employers have never encountered such on-demand access to labor market information. Yet *information anxiety* (Wurman 1989) overwhelms undergrads as college degrees fail to align with specific job titles, middle-class wages, or a sense of tenure. Selingo (2013) blames higher education's growing value gap and *sea of red ink* (p. 58) and Savickas (2019) surmises: "Work in the 21st century leaves people feeling anxious and insecure. Societal changes affecting employment continue to set an increasing number of workers adrift as they endeavor to chart their futures, shape their identities, and maintain relationships" (p. 3).

Efforts to improve education have devoted relatively few resources to providing quality career development (Bray, Reddy, Hurt, and Rauschenberger 2015). As the United States continues to have the highest college dropout rate in the industrialized world (Symonds, Schwartz, and Ferguson 2011) with students crippled by heavy loan debt, which has soared to $1.5 trillion (Federal Reserve Board 2019), strong efforts to reframe the role of career development in higher education is essential. With students carrying an average debt of $37,000, connecting postsecondary education to career development innovation and outcomes proposed by the T is critical.

Demand High for Career Development Innovation

Engaging learners in innovative and scalable career development to become T-professionals who can quickly adapt to innovation and rapid workplace change is a pressing concern to postsecondary and workforce leaders. This is especially urgent considering that the vast majority of students enter college expecting to gain preparation for the world of work. Yet only a third are confident they will graduate with the skills and knowledge to be successful in the job market (Strada-Gallup 2018).

Unfortunately, interest-only assessments, which dominate career development practice, have created an exposure bias leading to misguided advising and admissions practice (Feller 2018). The result exacerbates the consequences of a growing funding inequality, which splits public higher education into two separate and unequal tracks of elite and open-access public colleges. As Carnavale and colleagues (2018) posited elite public four-year colleges do not represent the populations they are supposed to serve. These observations shed light on why career development systems are urgently needed to create more diverse T-professional graduates ready for change.

Foundations of the HEROIC Narrative Assessment System

Narrative assessment, a relatively new concept, has been championed by many. This innovative approach draws from the work of Savickas's (2012) life design, Brott's (2001) storied approach, Cochran's (1997) narrative career counseling, Amundson's (2003) backswing metaphor, Mitchell, Levin, and Krumboltz's (1999) happenstance, Krieshok, Black, and McKay's (2009) limits of rational decision-making, Bright and Pryor (2005) and Bloch's (2005) chaos theory, Fredrickson's (2001) broaden and build, and Stebleton's (2010) strengths and limitations of narrative methods among others. Preparing graduates who can quickly adapt to innovation and rapid workplace change requires psychological capital (Luthens, Youssef, and Avolio 2015), immunity to change (Kegan and Lahey 2009), and growth mindsets (Dweck 2006). Building on these foundations and the need to develop one's self-advocacy voice and skills, Feller (2017) suggests adopting a HEROIC mindset as an information filter critical to navigating a lifetime of transitions.

Gupta and Govindarajan (2002) explain that mindsets evolve through a repetitive process, influenced by one's histories, positing changing mindsets means becoming explicitly conscious of them. "The more hidden and subconscious our cognitive filters, the greater the likelihood of rigidity" (p. 117). Limited in the ability to absorb and process information, learners create their own challenges with complexity, ambiguity, and information anxiety. Humans address this challenge through the process of filtration. Selective in that which is absorbed and biased in interpretation, adopting HEROIC mindset embracing filters of Hope, self-Efficacy, Resilience, Optimism, Intentional exploration, Curiosity and Clarity is encouraged. Adaptation is a key career development asset as Gardner states: "If you can't adapt your work to the context you're in, and you're limited within your own context, then you've got problems" (*The Chronicle of Higher Education* 2019, p. 38).

Facing a complex present and uncertain future, learners who embrace the word "career" as "the full expression of who you are and how you want to be in the world, which keeps on expanding as it naturally goes through cycles of stability and change" (Franklin 2014, p. 451) are greatly empowered. Within unpredictability, learning and maintaining self-supporting habits increase engagement during stress, disruption, and change. Without strong cognitive filters, "a person will be at the mercy of forces that he or she can't understand, let alone control" (Gardner 2007, p. 2). This definition of "career" and the HEROIC mindset described below offer concrete and positive filters for T-professionals as they look to thrive within complex, innovative, and boundary spanning environments.

Hope (H): A thinking process to actively pursue goals, bringing together will; a sense of investment and energy, and way; the resources used to generate viable avenues or pathways to finding purpose in work.

Self-Efficacy (E): A learner's sense of "I can" where they trust their own ability to organize and execute a course of action.

Resilience (R): Results from how a learner defines, reframes, and constructs meaning of events. Rigid or habitual self-defeating thinking limits bouncing back and moving ahead.

Optimism (O): The ability to seek solutions, see the upside of things gone wrong, and reduce the gap between present and future.

Intentional exploration (I): Looking for positive clues, taking inspired actions, and welcoming planned (and unplanned) opportunities as a way to grow.

Clarity and Curiosity (C): Possessing clear intentions and acting on purposeful commitments with curiosity, which creates focus, reduces distractions, and maximizes energy (Feller 2017). These assets fortify the emotional and cognitive flexibility needed for change, supply motivation to contribute and take risks, and reinforce commitments to move forward as T-professionals.

Sharpening the Career Development Filter to Move Forward

Recent and notable focus brings clarity to driving future career development systems. The Coalition for Career Development (2019) suggests five pillars for creating high-quality career development systems:

1. *Prioritizing career planning* to begin no later than middle school
2. *Providing professional career advising* with trained professionals to oversee this work
3. *Emphasizing applied and work-based learning* with business, government, and educators collaborating to scale a continuum of options, such as job shadows, internships, apprenticeships, and industry-recognized certifications
4. *Providing high-quality career development technology* to play a key role in helping students develop personal career and education plans
5. *Ensuring accountability* with rigorous implementation to confirm all students have access to quality career pathway programs and student supports (p. 5).

Four recommendations put forth by the International Centre for Career Development and Public Policy (2017) support (1) making career development programs relevant and effective, (2) identifying how work organizations are shaping career development systems, (3) ensuring the relevance of career professional training and development, and (4) building career development skills (p. 2).

Since postsecondary education and training offers tested pathways to middle-class earnings, observing new rules of the college and career success game is useful. Stanford's Challenge Success research (2018) documents that college engagement matters more than selectivity and most employers care little about college transcripts. This complements

Carnevale and Cheah's (2018) research as both studies demonstrate that the institution one attends for undergraduate education matters less than what learners do upon arrival.

Building a New System

Innovation within career development systems demands respecting the complexity of defining career success while honoring individual differences. Appreciating the internal dialog of learners while respecting their interpretation of past events demands clarifying six elements: personal qualities, strengths, desires, other people, assets, and natural interests using storytelling and intentionally exploration of possibilities within the HNAS framework. While engaging students in storytelling, we began to see growth in participation and positive affect. A pattern of elements, such as strengths, desires, and personal qualities are easily extracted from client stories as in the case of Lily (Franklin, Feller, and Yanar 2014), a college grad with a degree in cultural studies, and unhappily working in retail. Lily's desire for stimulating, engaging work, strengths in delegating and writing, and 100+ more items emerged from her narrative storytelling experience. This led to her writing a Career Statement, a key part of the HNAS. Lily used this written document to explore careers in advertising where she landed a job at a reputable marketing agency. Aware that helping professionals are a significant variable in the career discovery process, increasing standardization and reducing personality variables within the system could lead to evidence-based research necessary to evaluate a new system (Franklin, Yanar, and Feller 2015).

The HEROIC Narrative Assessment System

HNAS is driven by a framework (Figure 11.1) reinforcing the HEROIC mindset, gaining self-advocating voice and skills throughout and beyond the process. A two-stage process drives practice. In examining the HEROIC process, it is necessary to recognize that one's past story needs to be honored and one's future story will undergo stability and change. Identifying one's question in the left side of the top circle (Figure 11.1)

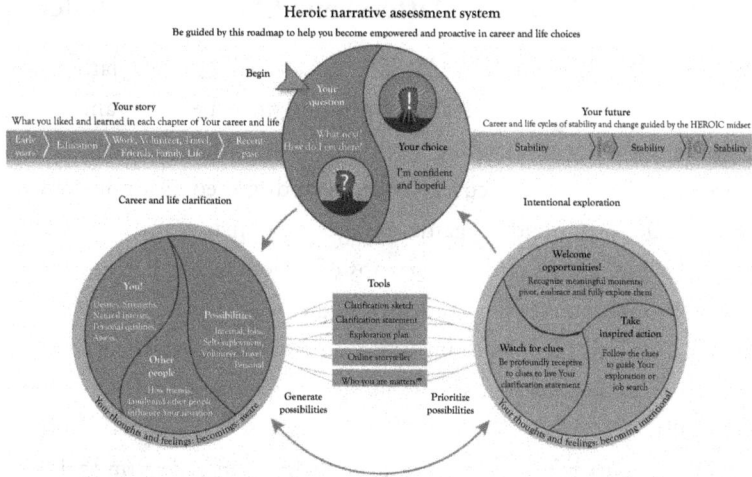

Heroic narrative assessment system
Be guided by this roadmap to help you become empowered and proactive in career and life choices

Figure 11.1 **HEROIC** *Narrative assessment system*

starts the process (e.g., *What should I do next? What possibilities are a better fit? How do I transition my past experiences into new opportunities?*)

Career and Life Clarification (Figure 11.1, bottom left circle) requires reflecting on past experiences to clarify the six elements: (1) *You, Other People, Possibilities, Watch for Clues, Welcome Opportunities*, and *Take Inspired Action*. Identifying the possibilities, one is curious about leads to creating a *Clarification Statement* later used to gain feedback and resources, take inspired actions, and identify a capability partner.

Intentional exploration (Figure 11.1, bottom right circle) moves clients to understand future possibilities before diving right in. This helps avoid investing time and resources before ensuring a possibility is a good fit to act upon. Tasking clients to *watch for clues* effectively reframes accessing labor market information.

When students engage in intentional storytelling, career and other helping professionals play a key role by listening deeply to identify important story elements. Generating meaningful career and life possibilities becomes an engaging and collaborative process linked to emotional intelligence, *essential skills* identification, and career readiness competencies (NACE, n.d.). This constructive narrative method aligns with life design principles (Savickas 2012), and exemplifies learning from a qualitative, postmodern career counseling lens (Franklin and Feller 2017).

The Who You Are Matters! and Online Storyteller

Who You Are Matters! (*WYAM*) is a fun, social, guided clarification exploration at the intersection of meaningful experience and work, personal lifestyle, and gaining a self-advocating voice. The energizing, peer-to-peer personal discovery experience disguised as a noncompetitive community-building game engages participants in this exploration. *WYAM* can be used with groups of various sizes (3 to more than 300). Though storytelling and meaningful conversations relevant to one's career and life a substantive document, a Clarification Sketch is created as a takeaway that strengthens participants' self-advocacy voice and skills.

Online Storyteller, a web application, helps users reflect on their stories and experiences in an organized way. The digital tool guides clients through the HNAS framework to define and clarify the six key elements listed earlier. Drawing from these elements, *Online Storyteller* supports generating meaningful future possibilities, leading to well-informed choices. Designed to be used collaboratively by helping professionals and their clients, or provided to individuals for self-directed narrative assessment, *Online Storyteller* allows for integration of other career assessments. For example, a client who gains insights such as idea generation, sequential reasoning, or spatial visualization from an aptitude assessment can add these to the Strengths section of their Clarification Sketch. Likewise, personality and temperament traits from frequently administered assessments can be added to the Personal Qualities section. Results from any RIASEC code-based tool can be added to Natural Interests.

Implementation Examples

Undergraduates are eager and capable of reflecting upon and creating meaning from their life stories and experiences. The HNAS builds on this potential and has demonstrated effectiveness across the life span with diverse populations, for both individuals and groups. *Who You Are Matters!* and *Online Storyteller* are used in credit-bearing and elective courses within higher education (Stebelton, Franklin, Lee, and Kaler, in press), as well as high schools, private practice, employment services, and organizations. Widely applied with undergraduate and graduate students from engineering to humanities, the tools have been integrated into a career course for the Canadian Medical Association, within a National Science Foundation program for doctoral and post-doc students at Colorado State University, and for graduate coursework at the University of Toronto titled "Engineering Careers: Theories and Strategies to Manage Your Career for the Future." Conestoga College includes WYAM and the *Online Storyteller* within over 20 sections of an undergraduate career class.

Saint Mary's University sought a framework to help undergraduates articulate a specific goal possibility linked to their deep disciplinary knowledge, but left the process open to personalized career coaching and students' changing needs and desires as they matured. Karen, the lead career coach, uses the HNAS to serve undergraduates by easily capturing the information generated from sessions and give students a specific goal of creating a career statement. The framework introduced systems thinking by verifying the clarification-then-exploration system, and revealing to students their boundary spanning abilities. Qualitative results showed that students liked the systems approach coupled with tangible takeaways flowing from their storytelling. Students and career support professionals found using HNAS an easier, more inspiring way for students to see their progress within the *Online Storyteller* web application, which placed the Clarification Sketch, Statement, Exploration Plan, and Getting Feedback in one place, clearly and simply laid out in an appealing mix of color and white space.

Karen's team all use HNAS and *Online Storyteller*, and report students' positive affect when they see a Clarification Sketch raise self-confidence (Franklin, Yanar, and Feller 2015). They find that when undergraduates have anytime and anywhere access to the web application, they have more ownership of their career development and information gathering process. Students with learning and attention disabilities have reported how easy this site makes the process of entering information and creating a career statement. Saint Mary's staff say *Online Storyteller* revolutionizes how they engage with students in exploring and telling their own stories.

Conclusion

With the fast-changing world of work, the adaptation and technical savvy of the T-professional is in demand and rewarded. Rather than aim toward a one-time occupational choice, undergraduates are best served by developing a deeper knowledge of the systems, skills, and abilities needed to work within and across disciplines as suggested by Gardner and Estry (2017).

Narrative, technology-enhanced, collaborative methods and tools trending in career development allow many practitioners to embrace new interventions. With few scalable, evidence-based systems existing to leverage narrative methods, which allow for integration of other assessments, the HNAS has demonstrated its value to higher education institutions seeking to foster adaptive innovation practices, boundary spanning collaborations, and comfort with complexity.

Digital tools that harness the richness of student stories and gamified tools that deeply engage and promote reflection offer promising potential to reach more learners while preserving the practitioners' professional judgment. With urgent needs for change in delivering career development, incorporating the HEROIC Narrative Assessment System offers great potential of bringing voice and self-advocacy to T-professionals. As postsecondary and workforce leaders seek efforts to accelerate and deliver concrete career development outcomes at scale they are encouraged to understand the power of using the *Who You Are Matters!* personal discovery game and *Online Storyteller*, which are outgrowths of the HEROIC Narrative Assessment System.

References

Amundson, N. E. (2003). Applying metaphors from physics to career/life issues. *Journal of Employment Counseling, 40*(4), 146.

Bloch, D. P. (2005). Complexity, chaos, and nonlinear dynamics: A new perspective on career development theory. *Career Development Quarterly, 53*(3), 194–207.

Bolles, R. (1978). *Three boxes of life*. Berkeley, CA: Ten Speed Press.

Botelho, T. (2019). *Personal Communication*. Retrieved from https://onelifetools.com/pages/simon-fraser-university-career-and-volunteer-services

Bray, J., Reddy, L., Hurt, P., & Rauschenberger, J. (2015). Transforming career counseling: Bridging school to career in the workforce of the future. SME, Manufacturing Skills Standards Council.

Bright, J. E., & Pryor, R. G. (2005). *The chaos theory of careers: A user's guide. Career Development Quarterly, 53*(4), 291–305.

Brott, P. E. (2001). The storied approach: A postmodern perspective for career counseling. *Career Development Quarterly, 49*(4), 304–313.

Carnavale, A., & Cheah, B. (2018). *Five Rules of the College and Career Game.* Retrieved from https://1gyhoq479ufd3yna29x7ubjn-wpengine.netdna-ssl. com/wp-content/uploads/Fiverules.pdf

Carnavale, A., Van Der Wert, M., Quinn, M., Strohl, J., & Repnikov, D. (2018). *Our Separate & Unequal Public Colleges: How Public Colleges Reinforce White Racial Privilege and Marginalize Black and Latino Students.* Retrieved from https://1gyhoq479ufd3yna29x7ubjn-wpengine.netdna-ssl.com/wp-content/ uploads/SAUStates_FR.pdf

Challenge Success. (2018, October). *A Fit Over Rankings.* Retrieved from https:// ed.stanford.edu/sites/default/files/challenge_success_white_paper_on_ college_amissions_10.1.2018-reduced.pdf

Coalition for Career Development. (2019, Spring). *Career Readiness for All.* Retrieved from https://ncda.org/aws/NCDA/asset_manager/get_file/308195? ver=385

Cochran, L. (1997). *Career counseling: A narrative approach.* Thousand Oaks, CA: Sage.

Dweck, C. (2006). *Mindset: The new psychology of success.* New York, NY: Random House.

Federal Reserve Board. (2019, January 18). *Consumer Credit Report.* Retrieved from https://www.federalreserve.gov/newsevents/pressreleases/other20190118a.htm

Feller, R. (2017, May). What is a HEROIC career mindset and how to have one? *The MCDA Wellspring May 2017.* Maryland Career Development Association. Retrieved from: https://mailchi.mp/7a4b643b7ed3/what-is-a-heroic-career-mindset-and-how-to-have-one

Feller, R. (2018). *Where's the talent? Employers and Communities Need More Than Passion.* Retrieved from https://forbes.com/sites/gradsoflife/2018/09/ 18/wheres-the-talentemployers-and-communities-need-more-than-passion/#4268c8565c24

Feller, R., & Whichard, J. (2005). *Knowledge nomads and the nervously employed: Workplace change and courageous career choices.* Austin, TX: Pro-Ed.

Franklin, M. (2014). *CareerCycles: A holistic and narrative method of practice.* In B. C. Shepard & P. S. Mani (Eds.), *Career Development Practice in Canada* (pp. 441–463). Toronto, Canada: CERIC.

Franklin, M., & Feller, R. (2017). One life tools framework: From clarification to intentional exploration with an east asian female. In L. Busacca & M. Rehfuss (Eds.), *Postmodern career counseling: A handbook of culture, context and cases*. Alexandria, VA: American Counseling Association.

Franklin, M., Feller, R., & Yanar, B. (2014). Narrative assessment tools for career and life clarification and intentional exploration: Lily's case study. *Career Planning and Adult Development Journal, 30*(4).

Franklin, M., & Feller. R. (2014). *Who you are matters!* Toronto, CA: Onelifetools.

Franklin, M., Yanar, B., Feller, R. (2015). Narrative method of practice increases curiosity exploration, psychological capital, and personal growth leading to career clarity: A retrospective outcome-study. *Canadian Journal of Career Development, 14*(2).

Fredrickson, B. L. (2001). The role of positive emotions in positive psychology: The Broaden and-build theory of positive emotions. *American Psychologist, 56*(3), 218.

Gardner, H. (2007). *Five minds for the future*. Cambridge, MA: Harvard Business School Press.

Gardner, P., & Estry, D. (2017). *A primer on the T-professional*. Lansing, MI: Michigan State University and the Collegiate Employment Research Institute.

Geisel, T. (1960). *Oh, the places you'll go!*. New York, NY: Random House.

Gupta, A. K., & Govindarajan, V. (2002). Cultivating a global mindset. *The Academy of Management Executive, 16*(1), 116–126.

International Centre for Career Development and Public Policy. (2017). At the crossroads. *Communique 2017*. Retrieved from http://iccdpp.org/wpcontent/uploads/2017/07/Communique2017-ICCDPP-050717.pdf

Kegan, R., & Lahey, L. (2009). *Immunity to change: How to overcome it and unlock the potential in yourself and your organization*. Boston: Harvard Business School Publishing.

Krieshok, T. S., Black, M. D., & McKay, R. A. (2009). Career decision making: The limits of rationality and the abundance of non-conscious processes. *Journal of Vocational Behavior, 75*(3), 275–290.

Luthans, F., Avolio, Bruce J., Avey, J. B., & Norman, S. M., (2007). Positive Psychological Capital: Measurement and Relationship with Performance and Satisfaction. *Leadership Institute Faculty Publications, 11*. 541–572. https://digitalcommons.unl.edu/leadershipfacpub/11

Luthens, F., Youssef-Morgan, C., & Avolio, B. (2015) *Psychological capital and beyond*. New York, NY: Oxford University Press.

Mitchell, K. E., Levin, S., & Krumboltz, J. D. (1999). Planned happenstance: Constructing unexpected career opportunities. *Journal of Counseling & Development, 77*(2), 115–124.

NACE. (n.d.). *Career Readiness Defined*. Retrieved from https://naceweb.org/careerreadiness/competencies/career-readiness-defined/

Savickas, M. L. (2012). Life design: A paradigm for career intervention in the 21st century. *Journal of Counseling and Development, 90*, 13–19. doi:10.1111/j.15566676.2012.00002.x

Savickas, M. L. (2019). *Career counseling*. Washington, D.C.: American Psychological Association.

Selingo, J. (2013). *College (un)bound: The future of higher education and what it means for students*. New York, NY: Houghton Mifflin Harcourt Publishing Company.

Stebleton, M. J. (2010). Narrative-based career counseling perspectives in times of change: An analysis of strengths and limitations. *Journal of Employment Counseling, 47*(2), 64–78. doi:10.1002/j.2161-1920.2010.tb00091.x

Stebleton, M.J., Franklin, M., Lee, C., & Kaler, L. S., (In press). Not just for undergraduates: examining a university narrative-based career management course for engineering graduate students. *Canadian Journal of Career Development*

Strada-Gallup. (2018, January). *2017 College Student Survey*. Retrieved from https://news.gallup.com/reports/225161/2017-strada-gallup-college-student-survey.aspx

Symonds, W.C. , Schwartz, R. B. & Ferguson, R. (2011). *Pathways to prosperity: Meeting the challenge of preparing young Americans for the 21st century*. Cambridge, MA: Harvard Graduate School of Education. *Connected life*. New York, NY: Simon & Schuster, Inc.

The Chronicle of Higher Education. (2017). *The future of work: How colleges can prepare students for the jobs ahead*. Washington, DC: Author.

The Chronicle of Higher Education. (2019). *Career-Ready Education: Beyond the Skills Gap, Tools and Tactics for An Evolving Economy*. Retrieved from https://illiad.library.colostate.edu/illiad/illiad.dll?Action=10&Form=75&Value=978556

Wurman, R. S. (1989). *Information anxiety*. New York, NY: Doubleday.

Contributed Author

Rich Feller Ph.D. is a professor at Colorado State University has served as president of the National Career Development Association, former coordinator of CSU's Counseling and Career Development program and Student Affairs in Higher Education programs. Consultant to NASA, UN, NFL, AARP, and organizations within 50 states and six continents, his publications include three books, six film series, over 100 articles and book chapters, and *Who You Are Matters!* Presently directing the Career Planning Program within the NSF's GAUSSI program he serves as chief advisor to YouScience, co-author of Pearson's Career Decision Making System, and career consultant to Semester at Sea.

Mark Franklin, M.Ed. leads CareerCycles, a career management practice, co-founded OneLifeTools.com, coauthored the narrative tools, Who You Are Matters!, and Online Storyteller, and teaches career management at the University of Toronto. In 2015, he received the Stu Conger Award for Leadership in Career Development. Mark consulted with hundreds of organizations in his earlier engineering career. Changing careers, Mark earned a masters in counseling psychology and career management fellow, and led student services initiatives in two of Canada's largest universities. Mark has authored or coauthored 15 book chapters, journal articles, and hosts the Career Buzz radio show and podcast illuminating career stories.

PART III

CHAPTER 12

Internships and Mentoring: The Keys to Sustaining a Healthy Talent Pipeline

Margaret Archer

In the book's opening chapter, the T-model adds two components that expand the conversation on the role of postsecondary education: (1) the importance of developing a deeper knowledge of the systems, skills, and abilities to work within and across disciplines and (2) a greater focus on the ME, the individual. One of the best ways industry can ensure growing T-talent is via internships and co-ops for undergrads, followed by on-the-job mentoring programs. Experiential learning programs satisfy conditions that promote both T-components outlined above. Internships and co-ops help students develop both the skills to survive and thrive in a complex, challenging workplace that requires a deeper knowledge of the systems, and the abilities to work within and across disciplines. In conjunction with internship programs, on-the-job mentoring offers interns and new hires the opportunity to explore and gain insight about themselves through coaching and feedback from an individual with vast workplace experience. This chapter focuses on two key dimensions of T-talent management: (1) the recruiting of students with T-traits into internship and co-op programs and (2) the development of interns and new hires by organizational mentors.

Excella is an organization dedicated to advancing T-talent through strong experiential learning opportunities for both current students and recent graduates. A technology company headquartered in Arlington, Virginia, Excella has a mission to work collaboratively with clients to solve their biggest challenges and evolve their thinking to help them prepare for tomorrow. They help organizations harness the power of technology to realize their future. Excella operates a remote development center in Blacksburg, Virginia, a location convenient to Virginia Tech and Radford Universities, where qualified students are provided part-time assignments and are mentored by experienced professionals in the best practices of software development.

Recruiters reading this chapter may find themselves naturally gravitating toward attending career fairs and campuswide recruiting events to identify talent. Through these activities recruiting teams may be able to assemble a large pool of possibly qualified candidates; however, Excella's observations raised concern that a focus on quantity over quality was not sustainable. Despite the high expenditures on college recruiting programs, the results regularly fail to identify candidates the emulate T-qualities, or if they do, the qualities are poorly developed. The recruiting process has been heavily weighed by the resume itself, with little emphasis on the actual person being recruited. When an organization prioritizes quantity over quality, the process of hiring becomes all about speed. Yet, to hire T-talent for an organization takes time evaluating potential candidates, crafting questions and assessments, and understanding what to look for in answers to those questions. To identify T-qualities, as well as a better match or fit between candidate and position or organization, one must go beyond the resume. Organizations need to employ a recruiting strategy that truly identifies the candidates for their needs, with the best potential for on-the-job growth. Finding and cultivating future employees who are skilled, motivated, dedicated, and positive contributors to the organization's vision is the main recruiting goal for most organizations.

Career Fairs and Recruiting Events: Finding T-talent

Career fairs and formal networking events are where the typical recruiter starts and for many years this recruiting approach served its purpose. Seeking T-talent—sought after candidates needed for today's complex workplace environment—require a change in the actual recruiting process. Recruiters must be careful not to fall into the trap of giving the company's "elevator pitch" to every student the moment they appear in front of them at a career fair. Instead, the recruiter should put candidates in a position to speak while they listen, intently. When meeting a student the first time, recruiters should ask questions that cannot possibly be answered with only *yes* or *no*. Instead, recruiters should ask T-seeking questions, such as: *What made you stop to talk? What interests you about our company?*

While this might sound like a fairly straightforward question, the intent is to search for initiative. The candidate response tells the recruiter whether the candidate has taken initiative to do research and whether they truly understand the nature of the company's work. For example, at Excella, candidates do not understand technology consulting as a career path.

What projects have you participated in that are relevant to the type of role the firm is offering? Most students might cite a standard project completed for a class assignment. The recruiter should ask questions that elicit depth and shows the candidate's ability to analyze and synthesize their experience and then relate to disparate situations. These examples could come out of extracurricular, work-related, or volunteer project as well as academic coursework. Responses showcase a student's ability to integrate depth of discipline, along with the ability to understand knowledge application and function within or across systems.

What is a problem you sought to solve through your work? This will give the recruiter insight into the candidate's understanding of the business problem being solved and is an indicator of their awareness of the world beyond their technical task.

What was the impact of the solution provided? Understanding impact on systems and processes well beyond their control is an indicator of being able to see the bigger picture.

Were there frequent changes in the project? How did these changes make you feel? This will give the recruiter insight into the candidate's ability to understand the perspective of others (or capacity for empathy), and the degree to which the candidate embraces change.

Tell me about an experience working in teams? What did you like or dislike about this experience? Few university students lack a teamwork experience they can cite. The recruiter should be paying attention to the likes and dislikes as they may contain an indication of the candidate's work preferences and capabilities.

Did you identify any issues with the work or project you were assigned? How did you troubleshoot your way through these issues? With this question, the recruiter seeks to determine if the candidate is thinking critically or simply performing per instructions, and how the candidate was able to pivot as the project morphed.

During a question-and-answer session similar to the one provided above, a recruiter is not only able to evaluate a candidate's ability to listen and understand the questions, but also gains a deeper sense of how the candidate communicates verbally, and the degree to which the candidate possesses T-abilities.

Motivators and Majors: Not What You Might Think

According to Smith (2014), 51 percent of students seeking internships report that full-time employment is the most important reason for completing the experience. If managed correctly, an internship program opens a major pipeline for talent. Excella's internship program sources its T-talent, which requires a careful and well-planned recruitment process. In Excella's experience, interns who seek full-time employment feel tremendous pressure to make the *right* decision when choosing their first job. Whether students are unsure about role, industry or whether they'll be able to pay their student loans with the income from their first job, they're weighing their decision. Thus, communicating their baseline technical competences are not always a priority in student's internship search. Often students are looking at the internship appointment to grow skills that enhance their major. Interns want to build T-skills—transferable attributes relevant across industries while at the same time they determine the career path they are truly passionate about. This causes an alignment gap in employer expectations and the entry-level competencies possessed by the student.

What does this mean for recruiting talent from college campuses? First, organizations should not limit their recruiting opportunities to a particular major. For instance, companies seeking software developers generally concentrate on majors from computer science and similar programs. Excella backed away from seeking talent solely from computer science, partially because they weren't meeting their talent needs, but also because some campus departments require company "membership" or sponsorship to have access to students from these areas. Additionally, despite recent efforts to improve gender diversity, Excella found computer science departments still lag in advancing women and first-generation students. Excella's recruiting efforts now include all engineering, business information technology, and other technical majors. Through this recruiting expansion effort, Excella witnessed an increase in gender diversity. Excella's internship program currently has more females than males enrolled in the program. Excella also found non–computer science majors to have a better balance of technical and nontechnical skills, stronger and more diverse communication skills, and a greater awareness of the business environment and their role in advancing the goals of the business.

Applications, Interviews and Hiring: Not Just the Typical Questions

Once the career fair is over, candidates wishing to apply for internships with an organization such as Excella may need to successfully engage with and pass through an Applicant Tracking System (ATS). The ATS requirements are fairly standard—upload a resume, which includes current GPA and occasionally a cover letter. Because an ATS cannot identify T-qualities, Excella goes back to their engagement with the candidate at the career fair—matching candidates who performed well with those that have applied. It is a coupling of both strategies to secure a qualified candidate pool. From these screening methods, Excella creates a pool of candidates and then moves on to Step 2.

Social skills and other T-qualities are essential to be successful in Excella's internship application process. These include verbal and written communication skills, confidence in their ability to contribute and take risks without being arrogant, and the ability to work well on a team of diverse skill sets and abilities. Step 2 in the screening process consists of Excella forwarding candidates a series of essay questions designed to further test their communication skills. Questions prompt the candidate to describe themselves in only a few words, talk about a challenging time in their life, or self-rate themselves on technical and other competencies.

In evaluating social skills, Excella's hiring processes benefit from a social component—one where candidates interact in groups to break down problems and come up with innovative solutions. Recruiter observations include candidates' capacity for empathy, ability to work as part of a team, and not be frustrated by failure, contribute and listen to other's contributions, and generally be easy to work with. Their ability to work as a team, whether that includes clients or staff from other departments will be enhanced through assignments that mutually develop depth and breadth abilities.

Teachability

Corporate organizations seek full-time employees with humility—a willingness and openness to learn new things and relearn things they might think they already know (Brandon 2017). Excella also refers to this as "teachability." Not always easy to determine, one method to tease out teachability is to have current employees, mentors in their area of expertise, participate in the interview process. During the interview, the mentor gives the candidate a problem to solve in their presence. The "problem" is designed to determine the candidate's skills in the area of expertise for the role as well as their ability and willingness to relearn. During this session, the mentor may instruct the candidate to speak out loud as they work through the problem. This allows the mentor to hear how the candidate thinks through a problem. It can also indicate whether the candidate has listening skills as some will fail to respond to the mentor's guidance or fail to speak their thoughts out loud. During this process, the mentor's observations should include the following:

- Does the candidate ask the mentor questions?
- Does the candidate make assumptions?
- Does the candidate take advice or feedback with grace?
- Does the candidate listen to what the interviewer is saying, or do they try to jump ahead and figure out what they think he or she is going to say before they say it?
- Is the candidate humble enough to ask for assistance when they're stuck or realize they don't know the answer?
- Is the candidate willing to admit they're wrong or will they try to debate their position with the interviewer?

Mentors

For the talent development program, Excella hires highly qualified software engineers with a passion for teaching and mentoring. Whether companies hire mentors externally or select mentors from their current team, selecting who will mentor interns, with responsibly for socializing them into the organization is an important role that should be thought through carefully and strategically. Before a firm embarks on hiring interns, they should already identify and define not only the scope of the interns' work, but more importantly the designated intern mentors. As one thinks through and determines the scope of the work, the following question can be used as a guide:

What role, task, or project(s) will the intern(s) be assigned? The answer will establish the scope of the assignment and ensure that the interns' contributions are meaningful, and the completed assignments will directly impact the organizations.

Identify the Mentors

Mentoring is challenging as well as rewarding, requiring patience, passion, communication and organization skills, preparation, and planning. Whether mentoring a brand new intern or a junior employee, mentors should consider everything they say and do, while continually evaluating whether they are demonstrating skills and traits they want the intern to learn. Mentors set an example for their interns. Based on the chapter author's experience, mentors must know their craft inside and out, be able to explain it down to the most minute detail, take nothing for granted in terms of the intern's knowledge on the topic, and always assume the intern wants the most thorough explanations. Excella learned that the best technicians do not always equal the best mentors. In other words, the intern should be carefully matched with a good mentor. Below are a few things to keep in mind when identifying mentors. A mentor should:

- possess T-qualities;
- be approachable and welcoming;

- not only be well-versed at their craft but someone who also enjoys passing on their hard and soft skills to a younger generation;
- be a good listener and communicator;
- understand that not everyone learns the same way and at the same pace, and is willing and able to flex for the intern's needs;
- possess skill level high enough to be seen as an "expert" by early career professionals they may be assigned to mentor; and
- have previous experience as a mentor, trainer, or teacher, whether in a professional or personal setting.

Below are a few red flags to be aware of when identifying potential mentors:

- A mentor candidate asking: "How much time will I really get to… (do my real job) ?"
- A mentor candidate impatient with the interview process itself. If a potential mentor is impatient with the interview process or the interviewer, it begs the question: "How will they respond to an inexperienced intern in need of their time?"
- A mentor candidate who doesn't seem to have a mentoring process or a standard way they convey a concept. This does not have to be a formal documented method, but good mentors know how to reach mentees struggling with a concept.
- Difficulty drawing conversation out of the mentor candidate during the interview process.

Consider the Mentor's Time

Excella designates 20 percent of the mentor's time to guiding and teaching interns or new hires. Mentors also use this time to better understand their intern's career and professional needs, which allows them to set appropriate goals and identify areas of focus. Excella provides mentors a modest budget they can use for coffee meetings and other activities to help cultivate the mentor–mentee relationship. Giving mentors this opportunity to speak with their mentee, outside the pressures of daily activity, enables the mentee to share work challenges they might not otherwise have time to express. These may be communication challenges or teamwork issues, allowing the mentor to further support their mentee in what is expected of them to achieve success.

Converting Interns to Full-Time Employees

One of the best ways to learn whether interns have full-time employee potential is listening. By listening, organizations can discover what their interns really want in an employer, what they expect from future employment, and what criteria they use to evaluate potential jobs beyond salary. This gives companies like Excella the best opportunity to "sell" their qualities based on alignment with candidate interests. To improve the odds of converting an intern to full-time employment companies should consider the following:

Give them real, meaningful work. No one, especially T-individuals want contrived, fictional work with a predetermined ending. Instead, they want to understand the bigger picture, know their role and opportunities for growth in skills that will span across industries and technical capabilities. Excella's goal is to get interns doing real work, as soon as possible.

Offer opportunities for professional and personal growth. Companies must work to create goals and development plans for their internship, co-op, or full-time, first-year talent. Helping these students or graduates understand their development isn't just about technical or hard skills, but in becoming a well-rounded (and T) employee that can contribute in different ways—from communication with stakeholders to performing with integrity and learning new skills. This allows room for not only the "work" but also the areas young talent are eager to explore. If interns feel an organization is interested in their growth and development, they'll be more apt to stay on in a full-time role, should the opportunity be offered to them.

Provide impactful experiences. Interns want to understand the work they're doing and know how it is making a difference for their client or a larger population. This is a key to their job satisfaction from the internship into a full-time employee experience. Thus, a company should make sure their interns, your potential future employees and leaders, under-stand their purpose. It gives them a sense of pride, not only in their own work but what their work has accomplished for others. Giving interns a view into the future of their role with a company, and how they can own a little piece of the company's success going forward, builds confidence in an intern's choice to accept a full-time opportunity, stay longer, and perform better.

References

Brandon, J. (2017). How to make yourself 'unoffendable' and teachable (yet still maintain your confidence). *Inc. Magazine*. Retrieved from: https://inc.com/john-brandon/how-to-make-yourself-unoffendable-and-teachable-yet-still-maintain-your-confiden.html.

Smith, J. (2014). Internship wish list: The 12 things students' value most. *Forbes Magazine*. Retrieved from: https://forbes.com/sites/jacquelynsmith/2014/01/08/internship-wish-list-the-12-things-students-value-most/#3709038c7b2f.

Contributed Author

Margaret Archer is the director of University Programs for Excella, a technology firm based in Arlington, Virginia. For the last seven years she has overseen Excella's Extension Center at Virginia Tech, ranked as the #3 Technology and Engineering Internship and #11 in the Top 100 Internships in the United States by Vault.com.

Excella Extension Center will become the *NextUp Exeleration Center* in early 2020, expanding to facilitate internships for organizations and con-nect them with skilled and highly motivated graduates.

CHAPTER 13

IBM: Being Essential, Transforming, and Getting Your Skills On

Jana Jenkins

As industries are transformed, reshaped, and interrupted, new jobs are being created that require different approaches to education, training, and hiring. Today's new roles necessitate a blended integration of domain knowledge, as well as digital, business, and soft skills—all areas of increasing importance (Eikenberg 2018). In fact, a recent LinkedIn study found 57 percent of leaders felt soft skills were more important than hard skills (Lewis 2019), which is concerning as recruiters are seeing a widening skills gap among job applicants, which may indicate an under appreciation of how critical these people skills are to business.

At IBM, T-inspired programs have been developed for employees to build these skills and gain domain knowledge through multiple channels. This chapter will more closely examine emerging IBM jobs and their required skills and provide an introduction into how IBM created a new approach to acquiring skills—one that can ultimately become part of a digital resume to share with potential employers and social venues (IfM, IBM 2008; Hall 2012; Moghaddam, Demirkan, and Spohrer 2018).

The value of T-professional is that they are interdisciplinary, instead of narrowly focused specialists. Although T-professionals possess deep specialty skills, they also sufficiently understand a broad range of related disciplines from which to identify contextual linkages, to constructively participate in interdisciplinary teams, and to continually adapt their contributions to rapidly changing conditions, scenarios, and business needs. A growth mindset (Dweck 2006) or the hunger for learning fed by a strong innate intellectual curiosity keep T-professionals striving for new skills development and personal growth. Opportunities to work with and possibly lead interdisciplinary teams requires strong social, negotiation, and communication skills to learn from and bring out the best from a group focused on solving problems.

IBM employees learn, grow, and impact the world in various and meaningful ways by participating in programs like the Corporate Service Corps (CSC). The CSC provides IBMers with high-quality leadership development, while delivering cutting-edge problem-solving for communities and organizations in emerging and mature markets (IBM 2019; Marquis and Moss Kanter 2009). The CSC empowers IBMers from different countries, with a range of skills to work at the intersection of business, technology, and society to implement community-driven economic development projects. This program uses IBM's problem-solving culture to help organizations address complex issues, while simultaneously strengthening employees' leadership and functional skills. Without strong T-minded professionals involved in CSC and similar initiatives, IBM's community impact wouldn't be as significant.

Don't Underestimate the Value of the Human

Another way of looking at the T-skill set is to consider the importance of social emotional learning. Studies indicate that early learning of social emotional skills can benefit academic success (Ashdown and Bernard 2012) and people with strong interpersonal skills, emotional intelligence, and social-emotional learning tend to be more successful, both professionally and personally. When we think of interpersonal skills, we find many are centered around communication, including verbal, written, listening, and questioning. People with good interpersonal skills tend to communicate more effectively and work well in a team or group. Interpersonal skills are therefore critical in work, in education, in social settings, and in life.

While hard skills focus on what you do—your ability to perform tasks within a specialization—soft skills reflect how you do them. Soft skills can indicate how easy it is for you to work with another person or group, how flexible you are when conditions change, and what your scope of reasoning is when making a decision.

According Lewis (2019), in his *The Most In-Demand Hard and Soft Skills of 2019* LinkedIn blog, the current, top soft skills include:

1. *Creativity*: People who can discern patterns, connect the dots, and explore new ways of doing things.
2. *Persuasion*: People who help others see value for themselves, consequently benefiting both parties.
3. *Collaboration*: The ability to work productively with others, with a positive attitude, cooperative spirit, and respect.
4. *Adaptability*: The ability to change course, alter actions, or approach to be successful.
5. *Time Management*: Process of organizing and planning how to divide your time between specific activities.

Power of Soft Skills and the Growth Mindset

Research conducted by Harvard University, the Carnegie Foundation, and Stanford Research Center concluded that 85 percent of job success comes from having well developed soft skills and people skills, and only 15 percent of job success comes from technical skills and knowledge (Eikenberg 2018). In the same study, 92 percent of recruiters said soft skills matter as much or more than hard skills when they hire, and 89 percent felt *bad hires* have poor soft skills.

At IBM, client satisfaction is a very important gauge of how our clients view the company, and soft skills have a direct effect on how our clients view support. Client satisfaction leads to stronger customer loyalty, which translates into improved revenues. Being recognized as having strong soft skills can be seen by demonstrating that you are:

- a good coach,
- a strong communicator, both verbal and written,
- insightful regarding others, including those with differing values and perspectives,
- an effective listener,
- a strong team player,
- a critical thinker,

- a problem-solver,
- a negotiator, and
- a connector of and across complex patterns and ideas (IBM 2018e).

The good news is that skills, such as those above, can be cultivated and enhanced. Soft skills are continually developed through practical application during one's approach toward everyday life and the workplace, and unlike hard skills, they are interpersonal and broadly applicable. At IBM, we help develop soft skills by encouraging our employees to have a growth mindset through offering digital badges to increase employees' applied skills. In fact, as part of the Digital Badge program, which will be explained later in more detail, there is an Open Badge–Skills Recognition series for building these skills. Having a growth mindset (Dweck 2015) means focusing on improving oneself and believing that individuals can develop and grow. At IBM, having a growth mindset is necessary for success, as its leaders believe commitment to continuous learning and growth is essential to thriving in an ever-changing environment.

The Growth Mindset

Individuals naturally differ, some more intelligent and others more adventurous, which can be attributed to each individual's combination of environment, physiology, and genetic makeup. But an individual's approach to the world, whether it be *fixed* or *growth* mindset (Dweck 2015; Hochanadel and Finamore 2015), can shape work behaviors. People with a *growth mindset* believe that they can improve or change their personality characteristics over time. They believe that the future offers opportunities to grow, even during challenging times. Fixed mindsets believe that their intelligence, personality, and character are inherent and static, locked, or fixed. Their potential is determined at birth or early on and it doesn't change. Folks with this mindset typically display the following characteristics:

- Avoid failure
- Have a strong desire to look smart

- Avoid challenges
- Stick to what they know
- Take feedback and criticism as personal
- Doesn't change or improve (Dweck 2009).

Individuals with growth mindsets believe their intelligence, personality, and character can be continuously developed. Their true potential is unknown and unknowable. People with this mindset typically display the following characteristics:

- Desire continuous learning
- Confront uncertainty
- Embrace challenges
- Are not afraid to fail
- Put a lot of effort into learning
- Consider feedback focused on current capabilities (Dweck 2009).

These characteristics point to employees who are open to continuous learning throughout their lives, working toward their true potential.

Adult Learning Theory

Adult learners are highly motivated to learn if they believe they can learn new, relevant content that subsequently helps them solve real problems that are a significant impediment, in either their professional or personal lives. In addition to the internal motivation to achieve goals, a strength of will comes into play when deciding to direct attention and focus on specific learning.

Adult learning theories offer a lens with which to understand the factors that shape our internal motivation. Pappas (2014) highlights four factors: (1) having a successful experience when learning, (2) exhibiting a sense of self-directedness for what we learn, (3) possessing the confidence that what we learn will be valuable in work and life, and (4) that what we do will be pleasurable and engaging.

Continuous support that employees require to be successful in this dynamic, evolving business environment starts at the top. IBM employees receive great leadership and vision from Diane Gherson, recently named the 2018 Human Resources Executive of the Year (PRLog 2018). One change Gherson and her team launched helps employees address the requirement of growing new skills faster, maximizing the time they have to learn, and identifying better ways of learning from others through the *Digital Badge Program* (IBM 2019d).

The Digital Badge Program

A *badge* is a digital representation of an outcome or achievement (Gibson et al. 2015). *Open Badges* refer specifically to digital credentials that adhere to an open standard being led by IMS Global Learning Consortium for recognizing and validating learning (IMS 2017; Glover and Latif 2013). The digital credentials are secure, web-enabled credentials that contain granular, verified information employers or clients can use to evaluate an individual's potential, capabilities, or skills. Key characteristics and benefits of digital credentials include the following:

- Symbolizes skills and achievements
- Contains metadata with skills tags and accomplishments
- Shares easily in social media: LinkedIn, Twitter, Facebook, blogs
- Builds the company brand in the market

Open Badges take advantage of the dominant trends in many economic sectors or industries like the IT industry, including cloud computing, social media, and Big Data. The combination of metadata, verification, and social media makes Open Badges even more powerful. For the learner, earning badges increases engagement and helps communicate ongoing learning and skills to the talent marketplace. For IBM, professionals who are highly skilled with their products bring value and results to their employers and customers.

Currently, IBM is adopting the Open Badges standard as an innovative way for IT professionals to validate their learning activities, skills, and achievements. Open Badges can be earned for completing courses, passing a certification exam, publishing externally (for example, books, blogs, white papers), and creating apps. For IBM, badges provides a faster way to push new skills into the marketplace rather than developing entirely new certificate or credentialing programs. Open Badges are certainly not exclusive to IBM. They are free to any organization for creating, issuing, and verifying digital badges (Mozilla Open Badges: http://openbadges.org/).

The Perfect Skill Set

One might argue that T-talent possess the perfect skill set. As an expert in one field, the T-professional can be counted on to successfully complete tasks in their area of expertise and work intelligently and productively with experts in other specialized fields. Their abilities save a company time and money because less effort is spent explaining things and more time is spent accomplishing things. If one's job description crosses several skill sets, as do many of today's roles and projects, then there is an obvious preference for, and absolute need for T-talent.

Tomorrow's workers will build their careers in a globally integrated, and constantly changing world, using smarter technologies to effect positive global change. This constant change will require the development and honing of new skills while leveraging personal skills, including emotional intelligence, to establish and foster relationships with others of complementary skill sets to collaboratively address the current challenges.

New Collar Jobs

Constant technological, industrial, and business changes affect the types of jobs available in the workplace and how they are filled. With so many vacant tech jobs, new ways to identify the qualified candidates is critical. It is an IBM problem; it is every employers' problem. The challenge is to close the skills gap. According to Ginny Rometty, IBM Chairman and CEO, it's about the relevancy of the skills versus the degree that become the qualifying characteristics of *new-collar* work (Rometty 2016; Ohm 2019). Typical new-collar jobs include: Cloud computing technicians, database managers, cybersecurity analysts, user interface designers, and various IT roles. These roles aren't white collar or blue collar jobs—they're new collar jobs, where skills matter the most. From coding camps, IBM pioneered P-TECH, and community colleges, new collar IBMers have built in-demand skills that qualify them to fill these important tech openings (IBM 2019b). The P-TECH 9-14 School Model is a pioneering education initiative created by IBM to prepare young talent with the academic, technical, and professional skills required for new-collar jobs. P-TECH represents the best of a dynamic public–private partnerships: students taking high school and college coursework simultaneously, while also engaging in industry-guided workforce development. P-TECH connects high school to college and college to career through an integrated curriculum augmented by one-on-one mentor support for each student, paid internships, workplace learning, and future career opportunities. With no admission screening, the inaugural school in Brooklyn, New York, serves low-income students of color and is the first P-TECH school to complete its full six years. It works! The school's college completion rates are 400 percent higher than the national average.

Developing the Individual

IBM is continually striving to make today's tech workforce more diverse and inclusive (IBM 2019c). Diversity is best reflected in the ways that its workforce professionals have built the skills required for success. The message of the value of skills and the need for rapid retraining has been communicated loudly and broadly throughout IBM. Employees are continuously learning new skills through IBM training sessions, expertise exchanges, and one-on-one skills development programs. When employees are offered personal development, goal achievement opportunities, and creative problem-solving tasks, they feel valued and engaged. Individual interests grow and evolve based on various factors, including vocation, career goals, and current or future work aspirations.

Fluidity of the business environment and rapid changes in technology are affecting and disrupting industries. These disruptions require new perspectives and practices in identifying and retaining talent and call for employees to continue to grow and learn, and in particular, master soft skills in recognition of the critical importance of being human. The T-individual with a set of "perfect skills" possesses deep technical or specialization skills as well as the proficiency and ability to lead, communicate, and collaborate (Spohrer 2014; T Academy 2018). But are they focusing on reinventing themselves in the right ways? Doing more is no longer the route to success. The PricewaterhouseCoopers report (PwC 2017) found that 86 percent of human soft skills will always be in demand. If individuals want to have and hone soft skills in an organization, being willing to give people time to cultivate the best in themselves is critical. This talent, spurred by a growth mindset, continually challenges personal development both vertically and horizontally, creating solutions essential to a Smarter Planet.

References

Ashdown, D. M., & Bernard, M. E. (2012). Can explicit instruction in social and emotional learning skills benefit the social-emotional development, well-being, and academic achievement of young children? *Early Childhood Education Journal, 39*(6), 397–405.

Dweck, C. (2006). *Mindset Website.* Retrieved from https://mindsetonline.com/abouttheauthor/

Dweck, C. (2015). Carol Dweck revisits the growth mindset. *Education Week, 35*(5), 20–24.

Eikenberg, D. (2018). Why soft skills are harder than they look. *Forbes Coaches Council.* Retrieved from https://forbes.com/sites/forbescoachescouncil/2018/07/12/why-soft-skills-are-harder-than-they-look/

Gibson, D., Ostashewski, N., Flintoff, K., Grant, S., & Knight, E. (2015). Digital badges in education. *Education and Information Technologies, 20*(2), 403–410.

Glover, I. & Latif, F. (2013). Investigating perceptions and potential of open badges in formal higher education. In *Association for the Advancement of Computing in Education (AACE), EdMedia+ Innovate Learning.* ResearchGate: https://researchgate.net/publication/266852980_Investigating_Perceptions_and_Potential_of_Open_Badges_in_Formal_Higher_Education/citation/download

Hall, S. (2012). What is T-shaped talent – and is it important? *IMeetCenteral, PGSi.* Retrieved from https://imeetcentral.com/what-is-t-shaped-talent-and-is-it-important

Hochanadel, A., & Finamore, D. (2015). Fixed and growth mindset in education and how grit helps students persist in the face of adversity. *Journal of International Education Research, 11*(1), 47–50.

IBM. (2018e). *Open Badges – Skills Recognition.* Retrieved from w3connections. ibm.com/wikis/home?lang=enus#!/wiki/zSystems%20Support%20 Onboarding%20and %20Training

IBM. (2019a). *Corporate Service Corps.* Retrieved from https://ibm.com/ibm/ responsibility/corporateservicecorps/

IBM. (2019b). *P-TECH: When Skills Meet Opportunity, Success Happens.* Retrieved from https://ibm.com/thought-leadership/ptech/index.html

IBM. (2019c). *I pledge to Be ... IBM Be Equal Initiative.* Retrieved from https:// ibm.com/thought-leadership/beequal/

IBM. (2019d). *Badges: What is an IBM Digital Badge?* Retrieved from https:// www-03.ibm.com/services/learning/ites.wss/zz-en?pageType=page&c=M42 5350C34234U21

IfM., & IBM. (2008). *Succeeding through service innovation: A service perspective for education, research, business, and government.* Cambridge, UK: University of Cambridge: Institute for Manufacturing.

IMS. (2017). Open badges transition FAQ. *IMS Global Learning Consortium.* Retrieved from http://developers.imsglobal.org/open-badges-transition-faq

Lewis. G. (2019). The most in-demand hard and soft skills of 2019. *LinkedIn Talent Blog.* Retrieved from https://business.linkedin.com/talent-solutions/ blog/trends-and-research/2018/the-most-in-demand-hard-and-soft-skills- of-2018

Marquis, C., & Moss Kanter, R. (2009). IBM: The corporate service corps. HBS Case No. 409-106. *Harvard Business School Organizational Behavior Unit.* Retrieved from https://papers.ssrn.com/sol3/papers.cfm?abstract_ id=1407558

Moghaddam, Y., Demirkan, H., & Spohrer, J. (2018). T-shaped professionals: Adaptive innovators. In J. Spohrer & H. Demirkan (Eds.), *Service systems and innovations in business and society collection.* New York, NY: Business Expert Press.

National Safety Council. (2019). *Fatigue - You Are More Than Just Tired.* Retrieved from https://nsc.org/work-safety/safety-topics/fatigue

Ohm, A. (2019). The best paying new collar jobs. *ZipRecruiter Blog.* Retrieved from https://ziprecruiter.com/blog/the-best-paying-new-collar-jobs/

Pappas, C. (2014). 9 Tips to apply adult learning theory to eLearning. *eLearningIndustry.* Retrieved from https://elearningindustry.com/9-tips- apply-adult-learning-theory-to-elearning

PRLog. (2018). *IBM's Diane Gherson Named 2018 HR Executive of the Year.* Retrieved from https://prlog.org/12735286-ibms-diane-gherson-named- 2018-hr-executive-of-the-year.html

PWC. (2017). Workforce of the future: The competing forces shaping 2030. *Price Waterhouse Consulting*. Retrieved from https://pwc.com/gx/en/services/people-organisation/workforce-of-the-future/workforce-of-the-future-the-competing-forces-shaping-2030-pwc.pdf

Rometty, G. (2016). IBM CEO Ginni Rometty's letter to the U.S. President-Elect. *Interpersonal Skills*. Retrieved from https://ibm.com/blogs/policy/ibm-ceo-ginni-romettys-letter-u-s-president-elect/SkillYouNeed

Spohrer, J. (2014). 21C talent and 21C citizens. *Jim Spohrer's Blog*. Retrieved from http://service-science.info/archives/3328

T Academy. (2018). What is the "T". *T Summit*. Retrieved from http://tsummit.org/t

Contributed Author

Jana Jenkins is currently a Technical Vitality Development Manager for IBM. She defines and leads technical career growth activities that support and demonstrate skill accomplishment and promotion readiness. She is a member of the IBM Academy of Technology and collaborates with technical leaders worldwide to address business challenges with inspired innovation. She is a creative problem-solver, who realized that the opportunity to contribute to the IBM patent portfolio was too good to miss. She has been an IBM Master Inventor for the past 12 years. Outside of work, she enjoys her family, her dog Reggie, and escaping to historical dramas.

CHAPTER 14

The T-leaders

Duncan Ferguson

Everyone has an opinion on leadership. Googling the word *leadership* produces almost four billion (that's right, *billion*) results. When it comes to how to lead younger generations of employees, there is certainly no shortage of thought. Googling *how to lead future workforce generations* gives us an unmanageable 63 million results. Amid all this chatter, leaders find themselves at a vexing junction where the demands of a dynamic and rapidly churning marketplace intersect with the evolving work, career, and life expectations of younger generations of workers. As you read in the last chapter, Hopkins declares Generation Z will live through a period of *intense and ongoing churn* in terms of workspace and team. Thus it will be necessary for their interpersonal skills to be extraordinary and their ability to handle change outstanding. This chapter will try to make sense of all this noise to prepare the leaders of today and tomorrow to successfully lead younger generations of top talent. It will also argue how a T-student will be well-positioned for leadership success.

Our Dynamic World

T-students who have leadership aspirations will enter a world where marketplace dynamics and accelerated technology advances have made everything faster, more complex, and increasingly diverse, a world where rapid change isn't the exception but the rule. In his presentation *Talking Talent and Leadership*, Tim Reynolds, Executive Director at Ohio University's Robert D. Walter Center for Strategic Leadership (2017), identified top marketplace trends that will impact the workplace, and ultimately leadership, over the next 20 years.

- Artificial intelligence (e.g. self-driving cars; job automation)
- Augmented reality
- Mass transportation
- E-currency
- Sustainable energy
- Online everywhere
- Customized everything
- Logistics
- Predictive analytics
- Diverse leadership teams
- Remote work
- Less conventional work designs
- Workforce generation gaps
- Continuous work

Warnings about these burgeoning challenges are seemingly every-where, as these article headlines exemplify:

- Digital Strategy—Understanding the Economics of Disrup-tion (McKinsey Consulting 2016)
- The Age of Automation Is Here—How to Navigate the World of Work (*Forbes* 2019)
- Robots Will Take Our Jobs—Better Plan Now Before It's Too Late (*The Guardian* 2018)
- An Agenda for the Future of Global Business (Harvard Busi-ness Review 2017)
- Unique Challenges of E-Commerce and How to Overcome Them (Finance Online 2018)

These business and industry trends place organizations in a constant state of flux. Long gone are the days of a static, five-year strategic plan. One senior executive put it succinctly in a quote from a Vantage Leader-ship Consulting blog post (2017) on the strategic challenges of the current business environment: "Our business model is constantly under attack." Such challenges will call on leaders to be more visionary, strategic, and deci-sive. But that won't be enough. To stay ahead of the curve, organizations will need to excel in the identification, development, and retention of top young talent. This invariably will impact how organizations view leadership and will create a mandate for a set of people leadership skills necessary for future leaders to drive success. A critical part of this equation is being influenced by the shifting demands of a younger generation of employees who are migrating to a new mindset about work, careers, and life.

A Different Career Mindset

There used to be an implied contract between you and your employer. You gave them your loyalty and in return the company provided security, benefits, and often, career longevity. An indelible connection existed between the individual and the organization. It wasn't perfect, but it was how the world worked and it provided some sense of balance.

Over the past three decades, this contract has disintegrated. The individual employee has felt the fallout of the rapidly evolving workplace. Demands are higher; resources are less; technology has made work–life balance a daily challenge; and change isn't something that needs to be managed, it just is. New words such as downsizing, rightsizing, restructuring, outsourcing, and redundancy have become commonplace in our work vocabulary.

These churning dynamics have transitioned younger generations to think differently about work and careers. Long-term loyalty has been replaced by a short-term free agent mentality. *One company, one career* is an antiquated notion today, where multiple companies and multiple careers is more the norm. Job hopping, which used to be a resume red flag, is now a proactive career planning strategy. This change in mindset was detected in a New York Times article titled "The Shifting Definition of Worker Loyalty" (2011):

> *Now many companies cannot or will not hold up their end of the bargain, so why should the employees hold up theirs? Given the opportunity, they'll take their skills and their portable 401(k)'s elsewhere.*

Younger generations now bring a different view of careers into the workplace. The quote below, from Matt, a recently-mentored, early-career professional, highlights this changed viewpoint:

I don't expect (or even want) to stay with the same company for my entire career so I need to build my portfolio of skills to make me marketable for my next job and company. I want a company that will invest in my learning and growth as a professional. And, in return, I will work as hard as I can.

This comment provides employers a glimpse of what it will take to retain and engage young and talented employees like Matt. He brings to the workplace a transient mentality, so for him an investment by his employer in his professional development and growth is mandatory for him to remain marketable in the working world. And, while he promises to perform today, he will not make any guarantees for tomorrow.

Other needs are surfacing among younger workers. CNBC (2018) asked 1,600 high-achieving college and high school students what they expected from work. These respondents, which potentially represent the thinking of the more than 60 million Gen Z (individuals born between 1996–2004) who will soon be flooding the workforce, prioritize a healthy work–life balance and high expectation of job fulfillment. Ernst and Young's (2015) study of Gen Z and younger Millennial employees found that it was important for them to feel that their ideas were valued and wanted to be recognized for their contributions.

The Intersection of Leadership, Market Demands, and Workforce Needs

The combination of hyped-up market forces and the emerging expectations of younger generations of workers is driving the need for specific people leadership competencies within organizations. Ernst & Young (2018) identified five key leader capabilities required for digital era success. Each of these capabilities had important people leadership elements, such as providing clarity and purpose, connecting people and possibilities, relating to others on a very human level and leading with true empathy and inclusivity.

Reynolds (2017) highlighted a listing of the most important competencies that will be required by leaders to sustain and engage the workforce of the future. His list included verbal and mindful conversations, communication with and through technology, feedback, diversity and inclusion, reflective time management, interpersonal skills, professionalism, data insight proficiency, ethical leadership, servant leadership/ inspiring others, cross-cultural understanding, leadership identity, and branding.

Critical leadership *competencies of the future* are echoed by many others. The Forbes Coaches Council (2017) identified 16 essential leadership skills of the future. This list included fearless agility, earning respect, selflessness, listening, humility, communication/soft skills, authenticity, understanding the individual, flexibility, clear vision, adaptability, learning quickly, cultural intelligence, change leadership and versatility, and committing to a clear vision. Fast Company (2017) also weighed in with their list, which includes *out-centric* leadership, collaboration, transparency, soft skill assessment, and emotional intelligence.

The Case for the T-leader

Take a quick scan of these chapters and other articles on the future of leadership and a theme becomes evident. Not only will individuals require time tested and deep leadership skills such as technical competence, strategic awareness, results orientation, and decision making, they will additionally need to excel at a broader set of competencies ranging from cultural awareness and diversity to teamwork and collaboration, emotional intelligence, and mindfulness. In other words, leaders will increasingly be expected to have depth *and* breadth. Think T-leadership. And who will be better positioned to take on these leadership roles than a T-college graduate?

Over the past decade, research has emphasized the need for today's young professionals to possess deep disciplinary knowledge along with a sharp ability to communicate across multiple levels. These T-professionals are and will continue to be in high demand for their ability to think diversely, collaborate, build relationships and span cultural boundaries both within and outside of their organizations. As we have discussed above, these individuals will enter the workforce with an established expectation of how they want to be led. They will also bring with them a requisite set of skills, competencies, and values that will lay the foundation for their future success as a leader.

From this, one could imply there is a need for a new set of leadership principles, one that focuses as much, if not more, emphasis on the person rather than the drive for results. Or maybe there are already a set of leadership behaviors and characteristics that have been and always will be vital when people are leading people, interacting with people and collaborating with people.

Lead Well LLC explored this in a recent study of best boss experiences (2015). This study invited people to respond to seven open questions about their best boss. The study generated three high-level insights, which are relevant for this discussion. First, relationships and characteristics were two critical elements that were essential in building a foundation, which allowed a leadership process to thrive. Relationships could be one-dimensional or multidimensional (e.g. collegial, personal, mentoring, learning partnership), but in every case a strong relationship between the best boss and the individual always existed. The relationship with the best boss had a powerful and lasting impact on self-confidence, personal development, sense of empowerment, performance (both quantitative and qualitative), and life perspective.

Second, five demonstrated behavioral components are present in each "best boss" leadership experience. A definition for each is provided below:

- *Leads from a higher purpose*—demonstrates a purpose beyond self-interest and a purpose beyond the organization that is put into action on behalf of the individual.
- *Activates potential*—observes values, acknowledges, and takes steps to activate the present and future potential of the individual.
- *Grants autonomy*—imparts knowledge, business acumen, and big picture thinking to the individual, establishes clear expectations and then creates an autonomous space for performance.
- *Provides pervasive feedback*—consistently provides multidimensional (i.e., constructive and reinforcing) feedback to the individual.
- *Encourages reasonable risk-taking to drive continual learning*—fuels reasonable risk-taking by allowing mistakes while promoting continual learning, growth, and development.

Third, these themes did not operate independently but were part of a leadership process working holistically in concert with each other to engage, motivate, develop, and drive superior performance.

Building a Contemporary Leadership Brand

Insights from The Best Boss Study (2017) provide a spotlight on the qualities that will help T-professionals become T-leaders. Here are some actions an individual can take to build his or her leadership brand:

- *Lead with your values*: Become a values-based leader who consistently places the needs of individuals ahead of the needs of themselves or the organization. Display a strong moral compass. Have compassion for your people and their lives. Assure them that performance expectations need not be at odds with integrity.
- *Understand your leadership brand*: Conduct your own survey or ask your organization to perform a 360-degree review. Ask for candid feedback from trusted friends and employees. What are the facts regarding your leadership style? What do you do well? Where can you improve? What key elements can your leadership offer an employer?
- *Continually develop your leadership offer*: Closing the biggest gaps between the type of leader you aspire to be and the type of leader you are today should be your primary focus. Start with one area for improvement. Get input on how to improve. Then solicit feedback on how you're doing. Once you've improved, move on to the next area for improvement. Great leaders display a host of characteristics foundational to forming great relationships with their direct reports: humility, authenticity, positivity, optimism, "can do" attitude, fairness, ethical, sense of humor, thoughtfulness, and thoroughness. At the core of these traits is respect. Do your best to incorporate some of these characteristics into your leadership style. And, remember, the age-old axiom—treat people how you would like to be treated.
- *Be transparent*: In a technological age where information has never been more accessible, hidden agendas and part truths

are likely to be uncovered. Leaders must foster trust to build a culture that will retain employees. Communicate an understandable vision and direction, set clear expectations, and be open about what is changing and why.

- *Create a feedback expectation*: Rather than always waiting for formal performance evaluations, make real-time feedback a routine part of the supervisor–report relationship. Try to balance sharing constructive, respectful criticism with providing positive recognition for work well done.

- *Have more consistent discussions*: Hold regular one-on-ones with your team members and ask some of the tougher questions so many leaders try to sidestep. What is important to you? What are you good at and where would you like to improve? What gives you energy? What can I or the organization do to better meet your needs?

- *Focus on developing people*: More than ever, younger generations within the workforce want to quickly learn, grow, and develop as professionals. A great leader today must help people understand the potential they possess. Then they must make it their mission to actualize it by building real developmental plans, supportively pushing direct reports out of their comfort zones, providing them opportunities to grow their skills, and advocating for them to perform to their best potential.

- *Connect to the whole person*: All people, but especially young and diverse talent, want to be thought of not just as employees, but as unique individuals. You must connect with your people on a deeper level, understanding that work is only one part of a rich life.

Learning About Leadership While on Campus

Do not wait until joining the workforce to start honing your leadership brand. ThoughtCo (2018) points out that students should take advantage of their college experiences to both learn about their current leadership offering and develop their skills for tomorrow:

- *Learn about leadership*: If offered, take a for credit leadership course on campus. Make an appointment to talk with professors to get their take on leadership. Find opportunities to meet with alumni to understand their current perspective on leadership issues in the marketplace. Attend networking events to broaden your leadership network.

- *Understand your current leadership brand*: Career centers offer personality and values assessment tools, such as the Meyers-Briggs, Hogan, and the 16PF. Analyze your leadership experience prior to starting college. Perhaps you had a part-time job, participated on a sports team, or got involved in volunteer activities or leadership role in a high school club. What kind of leadership roles did you play? What skills did you develop? How did these skills make you successful?

- *Get actual leadership experience*: The Thought Company, a premier reference site, offered a list of specific activities that will provide leadership experience (Lucier, 2018). This list included becoming a Residence Hall Advisor; running for student government; volunteering for a leadership role in a campus club, activity, or committee; taking a role on the student newspaper; getting involved with a community service project; working with a professor; or applying for an internship.

- *Ask for feedback on your leadership skills*: Making a habit of asking for feedback is an important step in your continued growth as a leader. Whenever you find yourself in leadership roles, look for constructive feedback on your skills and capabilities. Reach out to people you trust and ask them what you did well and where you might improve.

Conclusion

Leaders are confronted with an array of accelerating marketplace dynamics that were barely visible when the new millennium began. Leaders of today and tomorrow will be asked to manage the evolving needs of two constituents: the organization in which the work and the people that they lead. Leaders will be expected to manage less and lead more in an effort to retain and engage the top talent that will be required for organizational success. T-professionals should be well-positioned to successfully take on these leadership challenges. Whether you are a current leader or soon to be college grad with leadership aspirations, building a leadership brand around the skills, capabilities, and competencies discussed in this chapter will be critical in creating success for you, your organization and, perhaps most importantly, the people who work for you.

References

Dawson, A., Hirt, M., & Webb, A. (2016, April). Digital strategy: Recognizing the signs of economic disruption. *McKinsey & Company*. Retrieved from https://mckinsey.com/business-functions/strategy-and-corporate-finance/our-insights/digital-strategy-understanding-the-economics-of-disruption

Elliott, L. (2018, February). Robots will take our jobs. We better plan now before it's too late. *The Guardian*. Retrieved from https://theguardian.com/commentisfree/2018/feb/01/robots-take-our-jobs-amazon-go-seattle

Ernst & Young Global. (2018, September). Developing purpose driven leaders. *EYGM Limited*. Retrieved from https://ey.com/en_us/global-review/2018/developing-purpose-driven-leaders

Ernst & Young. (2015, June). Global generations: A global study on work-life challenges across generations. *EYGM Limited*. Retrieved from https://ey.com/Publication/vwLUAssets/Global_generations_study/$FILE/EY-global-generations-a-global-study-on-work-life-challenges-across-generations.pdf

Ferguson, D., & Scherer, J. (Fall, 2018). 5 Traits of a best boss. *Illinois CPA Society*. Retrieved from https://icpas.org/information/copy-desk/insight/article/fall-2018/5-traits-of-a-best-boss

Ferguson, D., Furcon, J., & Pristo, T. (2015, March). Best boss insights: For improving employee performance and development. *Vantage Leadership*. Retrieved from http://vantageleadership.com/wp-content/uploads/2015/07/Best-Boss-Insights-HR-Leader-Magazine-2015.pdf13

Forbes Coaches Council. (2017, December). 16 Essential leadership skills for the workforce of tomorrow. *Forbes*. Retrieved from https://forbes.com/sites/forbescoachescouncil/2017/12/27/16-essential-leadership-skills-for-the-workplace-of-tomorrow/#f94e28754cea

Korkki, P. (2011, April). The shifting definition of worker loyalty. *New York Times*. Retrieved from https://nytimes.com/2011/04/24/jobs/24search.html

Louie, A. (2018, September). 7 Unique e-commerce challenges and how to overcome them. *Finances Online*. Retrieved from https://financesonline.com/7-unique-ecommerce-challenges-overcome/

Lucier, K., (2018, January). Opportunities for leadership in college. *ThoughtCo*. Retrieved from https://thoughtco.com/opportunities-for-leadership-in-college-793360

Moran, G. (2017, August). Do's and don'ts of recruiting. *Fast Company*. Retrieved from https://fastcompany.com/40451582/7-skills-managers-will-need-in-2025

Nova, A. (2018, June). What young people expect from work. *CNBC Personal Finance*. Retrieved from https://cnbc.com/2018/06/21/what-young-people-expect-from-work.html

Reeves, M., & Harnoss, J. (2017, February). An agenda for the future of global business. *Harvard Business Review*. Retrieved from https://hbr.org/2017/02/an-agenda-for-the-future-of-global-business

Reynolds, T. (2017). *Talking Talent and Leadership*. TED Presentation.

Vantage Leadership Consulting. (2015, April). Our business model is under attack. *Vantage Talent Leadership*. Retrieved from https://vantageleadership.com/our-blog/business-model-attack/

Wyman, N. (2019, March). The age of automation is here: How to navigate the new world of work. *Forbes*. Retrieved from https://forbes.com/sites/nicholaswyman/2019/03/25/the-age-of-automation-is-here-how-to-navigate-the-new-world-of-work/#4f6634c94227

Contributed Author

Duncan Ferguson is a consultant who provides leadership development, executive and career coaching services to clients. He has worked for Chicago based Vantage Leadership Consulting and a global management consultancy, BPI group. Duncan has also held several senior level Human Resources positions with BP-Amoco and GATX Corporations. Duncan is currently studying what best boss experiences tell us about great leadership. He has had two articles published on this subject. Duncan received his undergraduate and graduate degrees from Michigan State University and is currently the Alumni Relations Board President for MSU's Graduate School of Human Resources and Labor Relations.

CHAPTER 15

Adapting the T for the Needs of Generation Z

Richard Hopkins, FIET

Conditions for Success of the T

The IT industry and other STEM-based professions place maximum value upon individuals who are both highly skilled at their technical area of expertise while simultaneously able to communicate natively with other specialists. This enables them to lead interdisciplinary teams and positions them well to reeducate themselves as technology advances. These people offer and apply deep wisdom in large, complex situations, often outside of their specialist "comfort zone." This is the sweet spot of a T-professional: an individual able to accomplish a desired outcome within or across systems and interact meaningfully with others who possess different disciplinary knowledge (Spohrer and Gardner 2017).

The T-professional has served the IT industry well for 30 years. High-ranking T-professionals earn titles such as Distinguished Engineer (DE) or Master Inventor (MI). T-professional skills are even required for the Chartered status (symbol of professional competence). For example, in the UK, three of the five areas of the Engineering Council's qualification for CEng (UK-SPEC 2016) focus on general T-skills (leadership, interpersonal skills, and ethical behavior) with only two focusing on engineering specialist skills. However, the individual can only derive value from the T if:

1. There is long-lived stability in terms of the roles and skills required to make complex change happen.

2. That people can expect to be rewarded by specializing in a single profession for much of their career.

3. That significant change is delivered through large segmented programs or projects consisting of many hundreds of specialists with a need to communicate with "nearby" roles.

For Generation Z (for reasons we will examine), these three criteria do not apply. Going forward, it is less obvious what value the traditional T-professional model is to either the individual, or the STEM industries. How must we adapt the T for it to be relevant to Generation Z?

Four Symbiotic Trends

Although the power of technology has and continues to increase exponentially, the nature of that change for the IT professional has been relatively predictable. Raw technological advancement was driven by Moore's Law (Moore 1965), and the pace of professional and system evolution was driven primarily by corporate tempo and structures (the quarter and the financial year).

Over the last decade, four symbiotic trends have merged to accelerate technological change:

1. The end of the second Artificial Intelligence winter. Watson, the first computer to win Jeopardy in 2011, followed by Google and Alpha Go, and the rise of Deep Learning (Markoff 2011).

2. The easy availability of big data sets and technologies for processing them. 2011 saw the launch of the Open Government Partnership, the creation of linkedscience.org, and the initial release of Hadoop (Apache Software Foundation 2011).

3. The lowering of the cost barriers to technological innovation and the redefinition of hardware and networks in software via Cloud. Amazon Web Services launched in 2006 and Netflix becoming first 100 percent corporate mover to cloud between 2008 and 2016 (Netflix 2019).

4. The increased ability to collaborate globally via Github and open source models. Github launched in 2008; by 2011 the exponential growth of Linux and Apache OSS made them the dominant force

behind World Wide Web; in 2012 Red Hat becomes the first open source company with $1 billion annual revenue (Clark 2012).

As a result of these four symbiotic trends, individuals or small groups are now able to make significant modifications to the technological landscape. Small teams of experts from widely disparate backgrounds but with a T-mindset can now collaborate globally from their home offices building sophisticated systems or processing huge data sets with minimal investment and global impact. These advancements have resulted in a revolution in the speed by which software can evolve.

Business Drivers

The waterfall style that dominated the delivery of complex IT and engineering projects for the period in which the T was developed is now rarely seen as fit for most projects. According to an industry survey by HP Enterprise (2015), agile is the new "normal" with two-thirds of industry survey respondents using it as their primary development method. This change in industry method has been enabled by the four trends identified in the previous section. The primary driver for the change has been the business need for companies to influence their consumers directly via IT. Companies are now expected to offer high-quality IT-driven experiences directly to their consumers. Unlike carefully controlled corporate environments, the resulting requirements or the sociotechnical impacts of such solutions are often poorly understood until the systems are in use, so multiple releases may be required to get to a pleasing solution. IBM executive Paul Papas memorably tweeted:

"The last best experience anyone has anywhere becomes the minimum expectation for the experience they want everywhere..."

These four symbiotic trends combined with business drivers have resulted in a much faster moving business and IT landscape for which traditional methods are poorly adapted.

What Stays the Same

Of course, not everything in the workplace environment is different for Generation Z. Human culture is generally resistant to fast, radical change, and human nature certainly does not change exponentially quickly! Basic communication, leadership, and assertiveness skills are just as important now as they were 30 years ago. Initial T-vertical foundation skills and T-horizontal overhead skills are necessary to ensure an individual thrives in the 21st century workplace. There will also exist the basic *hygiene* skills necessary to function in today's IT environment such as collaboration tools, productivity tools, and a basic understanding of the methods in use.

These very familiar elements of the T-professional remain constant. However, the next four sections examine necessary changes that will be needed to support Generation Z.

Individual's Skill Sets Will Need to Get Broader

Traditional programs or projects would have different T-professionals working on different areas of a complex change (such as the requirements, design, build, test, or deployment) dependent upon their skill. As they completed their work, they would hand over their work to the next T-professional who would take it further. In this environment, individuals who were T-professionals are valued because they tend to understand the needs of the upstream and downstream roles and would therefore improve quality and work collaboratively with their *neighbors*. This way of working, with multiple handoffs between T-professionals, was called *waterfall*.

Today's increase in pace in terms of producing and refining systems means that *handoffs* between requirements and design, design and development, development and test, test and operations and support, have to be eliminated. This is already the case in mature agile environments where the cultural and organizational barriers all along the lifecycle have been eliminated. This means that complex endeavors will be delivered via small increments with high degrees of automation by small teams that can do every task in the life cycle of delivery.

The T, with one main, lifecycle deep skill and a broad area of shallow ones becomes necessarily broader. While there will still be a need for lifecycle-deep skills, people may be expected to have three or more of them, plus an "overhead" skill to ensure they can all be fully occupied all the time. In addition to having more than one lifecycle skill, increased focus will be placed on time management and self-discipline.

Individuals Will Work in Constantly Changing Teams

The four symbiotic trends enumerated earlier have accelerated the ability to make complex IT changes via smaller incremental steps. The need to deliver value quickly to businesses is also reducing the expected duration of complex change. Generation Z will live through a period of intense and ongoing churn in terms of the context in which companies and teams will work. Thus it will be necessary for Gen Z to engage in frequent team-building and it will be even more important for them to be malleable.

Long-standing and stable mentoring relationships that have been highly effective at building traditional T-employees are likely to give way to reciprocal and peer-to-peer coaching that will be more amenable to a constantly changing environment. Key qualities that seem likely to emerge will be cooperation, team building, straight talking, coaching, and agreeableness.

There Will Be No Stability in the Middle of the "T"

An increasing requirement that is perhaps most difficult for the T to adjust to is the need for the employee to adjust *constantly* to new and unfamiliar situations and technologies. Typically, the deep part of the T could be relied upon to provide a career of relevance, growth, and promotion. This seems unlikely for Generation Z as many professional jobs have some or all elements that are Suitable for Machine Learning (SML). As a recent MIT report highlights occupations in most industries have at least some tasks that are SML and a few have all tasks that are highly SML. Furthermore, the posited unleashing ML potential will require significant redesign of the task content of jobs, as SML and non-SML duties within occupations become unbundled and rebundled (Brynjolfsson, Mitchell, and Rock 2018). The more predictable elements of the IT profession (e.g., technical support; low levels of specialism) are already SML.

The industry is already moving to broader forms where learning can be transferred to a new situation with minimal (or even zero) human supervised training. This new form of automation is likely to challenge many roles that take place in reasonably understood environments that do not require an in-depth understanding of human nature and responses.

However, as broader elements of a role become SML, there will inevitably be productivity-driven pressure to absorb new responsibilities and skills to ensure the individual is fully utilized within the team. The need is as much for mental resilience as it is about skills adaptation.

Maintaining personal confidence as the world changes will require employees to anticipate change and reeducate themselves in advance of the change. This will require the employee and employer to reserve significant time for ongoing reskilling of all employees on a permanent basis. Key new skills include self-starting learning, continuous curiosity, and a strong self-motivation to reinvent. An individual's T will constantly adapt in both the horizontal and vertical axes as elements of their skills portfolio are automated through technology and to fit the needs of new jobs.

Lifelong learning is already a term being used to describe this trend. Many employees invest (and indeed IBM *mandates*) around 40 hours of training per employee. There is significant anecdotal evidence, however, that to maintain strong skills in an environment like information technology an investment of 100 to 200 hours per year (one hour per working day) is more realistic (Simmons 2018).

The second biggest adaptation employees and the T will need to make is the ongoing demonetization and democratization of IT and the advance of Artificial Intelligence/Machine Learning (AI/ML). Those who can (and make the time to) absorb new skills and knowledge will be the ones that succeed. This requires the core vertical specialist element of the T to adapt as quickly and as constantly as the general element.

STEM professionals will increasingly find themselves working in areas where general AI will be necessary. This includes:

- working in chaotic, poorly bounded or understood environments (no obvious mental models) and
- roles requiring deep understanding of human nature and responses (Marr 2018).

- Key skills such as empathy will be increasingly important, along with the ability to work with AI/ML agents. The key skills required include problem-solving and asking the right questions.

New Skills Will be Required Across the Top of the "T"

Given this high level of required investment in lifelong learning, learning how to learn *efficiently* will become a significant differentiator among the generic skills, requiring individuals to proactively determine their best learning strategies. Learning mental models of adjacent skill areas, understanding common patterns, and transferring and applying knowledge between these patterns will become essential skills. Ironically it is precisely this capability that may well be exploited to broaden the capabilities of AI/ML, making it a very high-value skill indeed.

Key *general* skills at the top of the T are therefore likely to include the basics of automation, machine training, efficient learning strategies, and application of mental models.

It seems likely that as jobs change and the areas for SML grow, the need to understand and tackle unintended consequences will also require a significant investment in ethical thinking. While exponential technologies will undoubtedly enable us to tackle more complex and difficult problems, the human aspects also need to be considered.

What Can Academia and Industry Do?

Even with today's relatively straightforward T, the number of people who can grow both elements of the T to enable them to deal with the most difficult problems or situations is relatively small. Any enhancements to the model needs to be kept as simple as possible to maximize adoption and results. This chapter recommends the following three actions.

Focus on Soft Skills for Greater Resilience

The new pressure trends listed above correlate well to the Big Five categories of personality traits as illustrated in the Table 15.1 (Richard 2019):

Table 15.1 Big Five focus areas mapped to trends and traits to encourage in T

Trends	Big Five Personality Traits	Important Traits to Encourage in T
Existing T-model	Extraversion	Achieve balance
No core stability	Openness Neuroticism	Encourage intellectual curiosity, creativity, and a preference for novelty Reduce propensity to emotional stress while remaining focused
Ever changing teams	Agreeableness	Encouraging trust and compassion
Broader job roles	Conscientiousness	Encourage self-discipline and aim for outcomes

Tools have been developed to enable quick identification of these traits (e.g., Watson Personality Insights can use lexical analysis to identify traits from text). Making people aware of their traits and encouraging the right behaviors via coaching is likely to improve their ability to cope with the levels of change identified in this chapter and the role uncertainty caused by increased automation. In addition, the individual might be willing to temporarily share this information to those assembling teams to assist in the creation of cohesive and stable teams and to identify suitable *on the job* coaches.

Move to a *Sunburst* Representation of Skills

A Generation Z professional needs to be exploiting a useful deep core skill while developing the next. Developing *adjacent* skills might be the right answer, but to be an efficient member of a small team, then *overhead* skills or even radically new skills might be the right model for the individual. It is unlikely, however, that a single profession like IT architect, IT specialist, or project manager will form the whole of the *vertical* aspect of a career and it is more likely that two or three *strands* will be required at different levels of maturity.

In conventional T-careers, it has been typical for *big steps* to mark career progression (e.g., the OpenGroup certification or chartered engineer processes). In a model of continuous learning, improvement, and change, smaller steps are more appropriate. Organizations are therefore adopting granular digital qualification models that can be used to enable

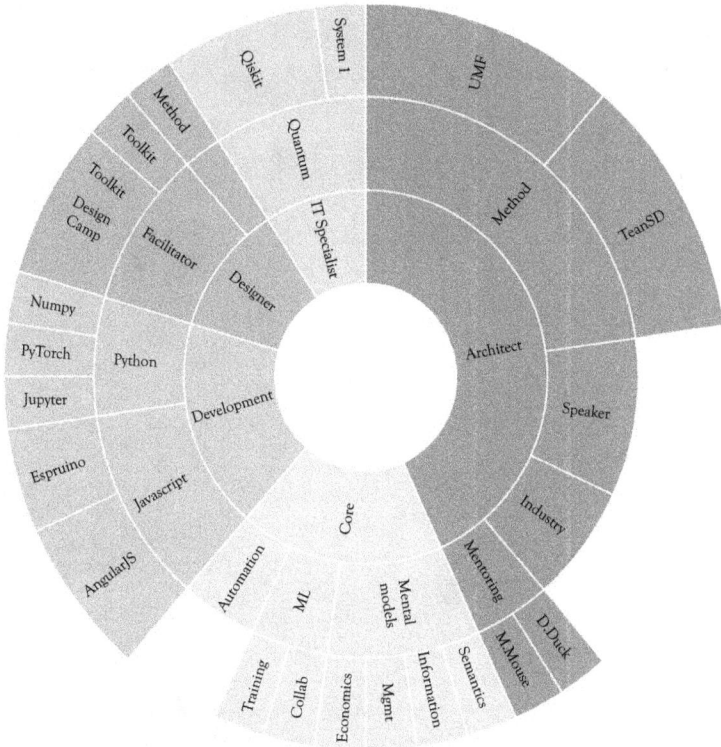

Figure 15.1 Sunburst representation of skills of a Generation Z "IT Architect" developing a second core skill as a Quantum ML expert

progression via smaller steps that *add up* to bigger ones, a representation sometimes known as a *star* model (Figure 15.1, Hopkins 2019).

A similar chart may be used to display the relative strength of personality traits.

Add a Continual Improvement Component to the Top of the T

The final enhancement would be to add some key generic skills to the top of the T that would enable the professional to continually improve their skills and capabilities throughout their career. These key elements include:

1. Broad knowledge of learning strategies (along with the personal awareness of what works for the individual)

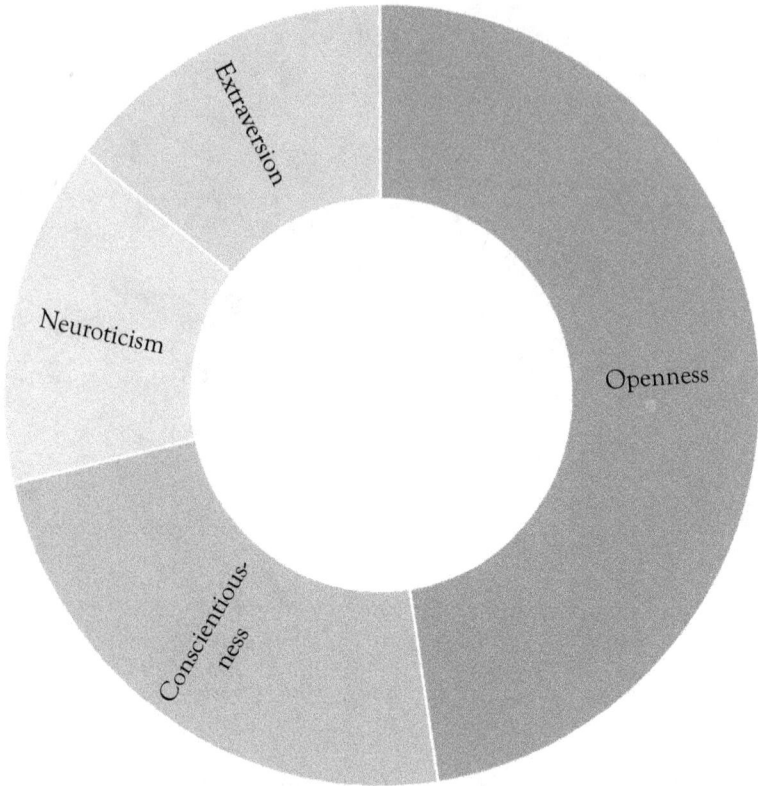

Figure 15.2 Relative strength of personality traits of an example Generation Z "IT Architect"

2. Automation techniques (helpful to deal with the breadth of roles being executed)
3. Machine training and collaboration techniques (the equivalent of today's ubiquitous productivity/collaboration tools)
4. Wide variety of mental models (to improve resilience to change)
5. A strong code of ethics on how to apply technology

Conclusion

It is clear the T-professional has provided a valuable model for 30 years. It has developed individuals and shaped professional standards that have helped deliver highly complex change. It has benefited both industry and the individual.

Generation Z and beyond are unlikely to benefit from the same level of professional stability and career predictability as that experienced by the last three generations. While the fundamentals of the T remain sound and necessary to enable teams to cohere and complex changes to be made, it is clear the T itself will need to adapt.

This chapter is a call for industry and academia to work together to create a refreshed T that can provide Generation Z the necessary emotional, as well as professional, capabilities to thrive in a world where the pace of change will inevitably continue to accelerate.

References

Gardner, E & Spohrer, J (2017) *T-Shaped Professionals*, Collegiate Employment Research Institute, Retrieved from http://.ceri.msu.edu/t-shaped-professionals/

Apache Software Foundation (2011), *release 1.0.0 available*, Retrieved from https://hadoop.apache.org/release/1.0.0.html

Brynjolfsson, Erik, Tom Mitchell, and Daniel Rock. (2018) *What Can Machines Learn, and What Does It Mean for Occupations and the Economy?* AEA Papers and Proceedings 108 pgs 43–47.

Version: Final published version, ISSN 2574-0768

Clark, J. (2012). Red Hat becomes first $1bn open-source company. *ZDNet.* Retrieved from https://zdnet.com/article/red-hat-becomes-first-1bn-open-source-company/

HP Enterprise. (2015). *Agile is the New Normal.* Retrieved from https://softwaretestinggenius.com/docs/4aa5-7619.pdf

Hopkins, R. (2019). *Will T-Shaped Professions Be Fit for Generation Z? (2 of 2).* Retrieved from https://w3connections.ibm.com/blogs/alt/entry/Are_T_shaped_professions_fit_for_Generation_Z_2_of_2?lang=en

Markoff, J. (2011). Computer wins on 'Jeopardy!': Trivial, it's not, *New York Times*, A1.

Marr, B. (2018). '7 job skills of the future (That AIs and robots can't do better than humans)'. *Forbes.* Retrieved from https://forbes.com/sites/bernardmarr/2018/08/06/7-job-skills-of-the-future-that-ais-and-robots-cant-do-better-than-humans/#763529c06c2e

Moore, G.E. (1965). Cramming more components onto integrated circuits, *Electronics, 38*(8).

Simmons, M. (2018). The math behind the 5-hour rule: Why you need to learn 1 hour per day just to stay relevant. *Accelerated Intelligence.* Retrieved from   https://medium.com/accelerated-intelligence/the-math-behind-the-5-hour-rule-why-you-need-to-learn-1-hour-per-day-just-to-stay-relevant-90007efe6861

UK-SPEC. (2016). UK Standard for Professional Engineering Competence (3rd ed). *Engineering Council.*

Contributed Author

Richard Hopkins is the President of IBM's Academy of Technology. This is the group that brings together over 750 of IBM's top technical leaders, including all of its Fellows. He is an IBM Distinguished Engineer and was appointed to this post thanks to his work leading large complex systems integration projects for IBM since the early 1990s. In 2018 he became an IBM Q Ambassador and teaches people how to use quantum computers. He has written extensively on complex systems integration, agile and semantic technologies, and has three patents in the area. His long-term hobby is building an autonomous robot dog.

Conclusion

Stretching Toward the Future

Doug Estry, Philip Gardner and Jim Spohrer

This book illustrates the T-model as a viable framework to create a strong, liberally educated college graduate who can adapt to and creatively innovate within a rapidly changing workplace. In a recent interview with *Fortune* that celebrated the 10-year release of *Change by Design*, Tim Brown, considered the father of the T in the United States, asserted the following imperative: to solve today's complex problems requires integrated whole-systems design, and an "understanding a problem at its most fundamental level, locating it within its broadest context, and mobilizing the fields of expertise necessary to tackle it" (Brown and Katz, 2019). Individuals designing solutions must think in terms of systems—the complex network social networks of meaning, behavior, and power—within which the problem lies. This means that problem-solving requires social and behavioral expertise as well as engineering, computer science, and business. With these few comments and not explicitly confirming the T, Brown stressed each of the major components of the T. The T-model provides a vibrant and exciting approach to preparing for a life whether professional, social, or personal, as all dimensions of our lives are becoming more complex, and more frequently disrupted by technology. To grapple with impending change requires each of us to have the abilities, mental mindset, and personal confidence to advance our lives and prosper.

An institution will not have to create anything new as the basic components of the T are found across campus. The deep disciplinary building block is well formed and successful in delivering core disciplinary mastery. Efforts proceed in furthering interdisciplinary learning but faculty struggle to understand what learning in an interdisciplinary environment means or how it should be enacted, strengthening this block. Institutions have been chasing the boundary spanning block for two decades with modest success in incorporating key competencies such as teamwork, cultural awareness, and interpersonal communication. Reaching the end point; however, remains elusive as the workplace changes faster than do institutions. The ME block permeates through campus in a variety of ways but seldom are a student's experiences integrated effectively so they can relate their T-story. Finally, the absence of the systems component in some learning environments makes it more difficult for students to understand and apply their learning. These latter two blocks present the biggest challenges and opportunities to activate fully the T-model.

Multiple agents, both on and off campus, will be involved in developing T-talent. The usual approach to reforming learning centers on the faculty and student dyads, which are typically faculty driven. Under T-initiatives, faculty will need to collaborate and coordinate with professional staff and nonacademic organizational representatives to create contexts that advance T-learning. Barriers will have to be lowered. Institutions will act as a system where through leadership, models of how the parts of the system should work together are created, rewarding those that do and holding those that don't accountable. A system committed to developing T's will require the leaders of the system to articulate a holistic T-strategy and support with resources, rewards, and consistency in messaging while the programs percolate up through interdisciplinary and inter-professional exchanges of expertise, resources, and understanding.

Artificial intelligence plays a strong role in establishing the urgency to develop college students as T's: they will regularly experience its disruptions. The phases of AI when overlaying the figure of the T draws attention to the dynamic synergy between the two. The initial phase of AI, which society had nearly passed through at this point, is considered narrow as these applications focus on specific tasks or processes, which have required deep disciplinary knowledge to develop. The narrow phase represents deep vertical alignment with the T. In the broad AI phase, where society is now, AI will have broader cognitive abilities that undertake tasks more like humans, including flexible problem-solving, reasoning, and thinking abstractly. As broad AI advance, AI systems will begin to expand horizontally over the T, requiring capability to interact and collaborate with multiple tasks and systems. The final stage, which is several decades in our future, will see AI general intelligence and superintelligence applications that can some perform some human cognitive tasks better than people as well as augment people to perform at much higher levels on some tasks than we do today. At this point, AI will completely overlay the T (for more details see Webb 2019). Richard Hopkin's chapter in this book argues persuasively that the T will soon morph into a more complicated model in order to keep up with transforming AI, which is already here.

The T-model offers higher education institutions opportunities to address challenges of preparing students for workplace without forsaking institutions' core values and mission. Brown is not sure schools are up to the challenge because they have been designed to "meet challenges that are no longer relevant." Institutions of higher education must play a critical role in this process as it provides the deep disciplinary knowledge, the essence of being educated. At the same time, higher education must keep pace with our rapidly changing and increasingly complex society. The corporate sector must also step up its game by investing in all the best and most meaningful ways to achieve the outcome they are so willing to tell everyone they desire. Thus, we must act as a system, moving away from lip service and fingerpointing, to work together to strive for a more cohesive-driven model. To move forward, institutions will have to display courage to overcome traditional barriers and establish new mindsets. They can be assisted by being:

- *Innovative*: open to creative ways to stimulate learning through curriculum design, technology, and space utilization that reaches in partnership with organizations outside higher education.
- *Intentional*: embrace T-learning as everyone's responsibility by being open and collaborative across disciplines and professional support units as piecemeal, ad hoc approaches seldom work or last, including noncampus agents.
- *Integrative*: practice reflection, storytelling, and other devices to assist students in the integration of all their experiences.

The T-model is not composed of separate, unconnected events. Rather the T is a system and requires practices to ensure students can understand how they can develop to become T-professionals.

References

Brown T., & Katz, B. (2019 March 1). The new blueprint. *Fortune*, 93–95.
Webb, A. (2019). *The big nine.* New York: PublicAffairs.

Contributed Author

Doug Estry, PhD., served as Associate Provost for Undergraduate Education and Dean of Undergraduate Studies at Michigan State University. In this role he was responsible for overseeing university-level undergraduate initiatives that support and enhance the undergraduate learning experience. He also served as Graduate Director and subsequently Program Director of the BLD Program and as the Associate Dean for Student and Academic Affairs in the College of Natural Science. During his tenure as Associate Dean, he focused on issues of teaching and learning in science and mathematics including work to advance a culture of learning outcomes assessment.

Philip Gardner, Ph.D., leads the Collegiate Employment Research Institute at Michigan State University. For 34 years, the institute has pursued research focused on the transition from college to work, early socialization in the workplace, national labor market trends from new college graduates, and experiential education (especially internships and cooperative education). Phil initiated work on the T-model 10 years ago and is a strong advocate for the model as a means to reimagine undergraduate education. His collaboration with Jim Spohrer at IBM and Doug Estry at MSU has advanced our conceptualization and practice of the T-model and brought a wider understanding through three T-summits. He served as a Fulbright Specialist to New Zealand in work-integrated learning; recognized by the Cooperative Education and Internship Association and the World Association of Cooperative Education for his research in understanding and leadership in advancing work-integrated learning. He was recently elected to the Academy of Fellows of the National Association of Colleges and Employers.

Jim Spohrer directs IBM's open source Artificial Intelligence (AI) efforts in IBM's Open Technologies Group with a focus on open source developer and data science ecosystems. Previously at IBM, he led Global University Programs, co-founded Almaden Service Research, and was CTO of the Venture Capital Group. After his MIT B.S. in physics, he developed speech recognition systems at Verbex, an Exxon company, before receiving his Yale Ph.D. in computer science/artificial intelligence. In the 1990s, he attained Apple Computers' Distinguished Engineer Scientist and Technology title for next generation learning platforms. With over 90 publications and nine patents, he won the Gummesson Service Research award, Vargo and Lusch Service-Dominant Logic award, Daniel Berg Service Systems award, and a PICMET Fellow for advancing service science.

About the Authors

Philip Gardner, Ph.D., leads the Collegiate Employment Research Institute at Michigan State University (MSU). For 34 years, the institute has pursued research focused on the transition from college to work, early socialization in the workplace, national labor market trends from new college graduates, and experiential education (especially internships and cooperative education). Phil initiated work on the T-model 10 years ago and is a strong advocate for the model as a means to reimagine undergraduate education. His collaboration with Jim Spohrer at IBM and Doug Estry at the MSU has advanced our conceptualization and practice of the T-model and brought a wider understanding through three T-summits. He served as a Fulbright Specialist to New Zealand in work-integrated learning; recognized by the Cooperative Education and Internship Association and the World Association of Cooperative Education for his research in understanding and leadership in advancing work-integrated learning. He was recently elected to the Academy of Fellows of the National Association of Colleges and Employers.

Heather Maietta, EdD is an Associate Professor in the Doctorate of Higher Education Leadership at Regis college. Her research areas include college to workforce readiness and transition; first generation doctoral student persistence and completion; and transfer students (particularly those forced to transfer due to college closures). Heather is a Board Certified Coach who maintains a successful career and executive coaching practice careerinprogress.com where she has consulted for organizations such as Stanford, the Kraft Group, Johnson & Johnson, Florida International, University of Texas, 3M, Marriott, and Staples to name a few.

Index

www.ingramcontent.com/pod-product-compliance
Lightning Source LLC
Chambersburg PA
CBHW061156220326
41599CB00025B/4507